A Psychology of Spiritual Healing

A
Psychology
of
Spiritual Healing

EUGENE TAYLOR

Chrysalis Books
Imprint of the Swedenborg Foundation
West Chester, Pennsylvania

Chrysalis Books is an imprint of the Swedenborg Foundation, Inc.
For more information, contact:
Chrysalis Books
The Swedenborg Foundation
320 N. Church Street
West Chester, PA 19380

Library of Congress Cataloging-in-Publication Data

Taylor, Eugene
   A psychology of spiritual healing / Eugene Taylor.
     p.   cm.
   Includes bibliographical references and index.
   ISBN 0–87785–375–4
   1. Spiritual healing—Psychology.
   2. Swedenborg, Emanuel, 1688–1772.
  I. Title.
   BL65.M4T33 1997
   615.8'52—dc21   97–18275
                                       CIP

Edited by Mary Lou Bertucci
Designed by QX+Company, Haddon Heights, New Jersey
Typeset in Janson and Bernhard Modern by Sans Serif, Saline, Michigan

To my Texas friends, Larry and Barbie Dossey,
and
Jeanne Achterberg and Frank Lawlis,
pioneers in the new mind-body medicine

and

to my compatriot and colleague at
Harvard Medical School,
Herbert Benson,
who preceded even these new voices
with his discovery of
the Relaxation Response

℟ *Jesus said unto the disciples,*
  these signs shall follow them that believe;
  in my name they shall cast out demons,
  they shall speak with new tongues;
  they shall take up serpents;
  if they drink any deadly thing, it shall not hurt them;
  they shall lay hands on the infirm, and they shall recover.
  And they went out and preached everywhere,
  the Lord working with them by signs following.

Mark 16:17–20

Contents

Acknowledgments

The present text first materialized as an unpublished manuscript entitled "The Psychology of Inner Experience" in the spring of 1968. It was then presented as a series of public lectures in the fall of 1975 at the School of Continuing Education of Southern Methodist University in Dallas. For that opportunity, I extend my belated thanks to the late Dean Mary Miller.

The contents of the work became significantly sharpened and refocused when I reinterpreted its main thesis as the fifth annual Wilfred Gould Rice Memorial Lecture on Psychology and Religion, delivered at the Swedenborg Chapel in Cambridge, Massachusetts, for the Swedenborg Society at Harvard-Radcliffe on June 5, 1995. For this opportunity, I owe a debt of gratitude to the Rev. F. Bob Tafel, Mrs. Wilfred Gould Rice, and the board of the Swedenborg Chapel.

I am particularly grateful to my various correspondents, both named and unnamed, for written permission to publish their personal experiences, particularly the Jungian analyst Dr. James A. Hall. The Rev. Leonard Fox, a minister of the Lord's New Church, provided invaluable materials on homeopathy from Swedenborgian literature in the nineteenth century, and Dr. Janet Piedilato provided a status report on scientific understanding of the hypnagogic state. Amy Reichert, Katherine Dimancescu, and Mary Katherine Duggan also read early drafts with a keen eye for important corrections.

Finally, I would like to thank my publisher, especially those individuals who have encouraged this work and who saw it through the production process: Rev. Dr. James Lawrence of the Publications Committee, a staunch ally of my proposal; and members of the Foundation staff, particularly Dr. David Eller, Susan Picard, Mary Lou Bertucci, and Kathleen Wasong for their keen efforts to bring this manuscript to the attention of the general public.

Introduction

This is a profoundly personal document, in that it brings to fruition a project on the psychology of inner experience that has been in progress for almost thirty years. It has evolved as the result of my wide reading in Western psychology and psychiatry; an intense period of supervised psychotherapeutic practice in both a university counseling service and various church settings; a four-year scientific experiment on meditation involving some 250 subjects, overlaid by a ten-year exploration of non-Western cultures, numerous personal accounts of interior experiences shared by friends, colleagues, and students, and my own journey of interior exploration.[1]

While I intend this work to be a contribution to the literature on psychology and spirituality, it is also meant to be existential and phenomenological—that is, wholly generated out of my own world view—and makes no pretense at being either a formal academic treatise or a scientific analysis. For this reason, I have kept footnotes, references, and personal identities to a minimum. Rather, the text purports to outline an experiential psychology of self-realization; it is simply meant to be a statement about the human condition as I see it.

The origins of this project date back to certain visionary experiences I had as a young boy growing up in the suburbs of Philadelphia and later as a college student in the 1960s, attempting to find the path I would follow as a life work. Such visionary experiences were a periodic occurrence of my early life, which I attribute to the inordinate Celtic influence of my Irish mother and the wide reading of my Teutonic father; my own natural, introverted suggestibility; and sequelae from brain surgery at the age of eighteen months. I had contracted cerebral meningitis and was a subject in a scientific experiment employing the first clinical trials of streptomycin. The surgery, from what I was told later, was exploratory and occurred in the recovery phase of the illness. I have always thought that the doctors left a surgical sponge in my brain, which would account for the ceaseless sopping up of information and points of view during my subsequent learning experiences.

My views have also been heavily influenced by an eclectic religious background. While I was growing up, it was always clear to me that my mother had been raised as an Irish Catholic. However, I thought that my father's religion was that of the U. S. Marines, since his four years in the military during World War II had such a profound influence on his outlook. Actually, his family came from a Calvinist and German Lutheran background, but he attended a Baptist Sunday school across the street from his home as a matter of convenience. My sister and brothers and I attended a series of Episcopal churches, and when we were old enough to decide our religious affiliations for ourselves, we all went our separate ways.

I ended up at Southern Methodist University (SMU) in Dallas, where I studied biology and psychology, conducted a number of experiments on meditation, interned in psychotherapy through the university counseling center, and worked for a Presbyterian social agency counseling young adults and their families. I also attended SMU's Perkins School of Theology where I studied Hinduism and Buddhism. During those years, I was associated mainly with the Unitarians, through their minister's pastoral-counseling and religious-education programs. Through several intellectual relationships with women friends, one of whom, Dr. Florence Wiedemann, was particularly influential, I also became enamored with C. G. Jung's ideas about consciousness. Subsequently, I found Jung's theories useful as a bridge between Anglo-American and Asian forms of psychology.[2]

On the Anglo-American side, I had been exposed to psychophysics and academic behaviorism as well as to certain forms of psychodynamic depth-psychology; on the Asian side, I became a specialist in Samkhya yoga and Indian Mahayana Buddhism. I had also immersed myself in what I soon came to regard as classical Eastern psychology, referring to the classical periods of selected religious and philosophical traditions from India, China, Tibet, and Japan. These interests led me into practicing *hatha* and *nadi* yoga under Kumar Pallana; into training in the north Indian classical music tradition under Pundit Lalmani Mishra; and into the Japanese martial art of aikido, the way of harmony with energy, whose goal is universal disarmament and world peace. I have pursued aikido to the rank of third-degree back belt, as a student of William Sosa, Koichi Tohei, Robert Nadeau, and Matsunari Kanai. I was also influenced by the writings of Jidhu Krishnamurti, then still living, whose charismatic thoughts opened my mind to the possibility of spiritual freedom.

During this period—the late 1960s—through the personality theorist and parapsychologist Gardner Murphy, I also became associated with humanistic and transpersonal psychology, the so-called third and fourth force in American psychology, which had recently emerged as an alternative to the schools of psychoanalysis and behaviorism then prevailing in academic and clinical circles. Humanistic psychology presented a picture of the self-actualizing personality; it emphasized the growth-oriented dimension of consciousness and focused on the existential nature of the psychotherapeutic hour. Transpersonal psychology has focused almost exclusively on spirituality and altered states of consciousness, largely from a devotional and quasi-scientific standpoint.

Murphy introduced me to Anthony Sutich, California psychotherapist and cofounder with Abraham Maslow of both the *Journal of Humanistic Psychology* and the *Journal of Transpersonal Psychology*. Sutich, in turn, introduced me to some of the younger psychologists of the humanistic and transpersonal movement, among them, Robert Frager, James Fadiman, and Miles Vich, with whom I have maintained a friendly association for almost a quarter of a century. Since then I have remained enamored with humanistic and transpersonal psychology, on many occasions have critiqued these developments, and several times have attempted my own definition of these fields.[3] More recently I have embarked on their detailed history, although I have never been a follower of the younger theorists now in vogue.

After leaving Texas in 1977, I studied at Harvard Divinity School, where I was admitted under Ralph Waldo Emerson's old classification as a resident graduate. In 1821, the year Emerson was graduated and before a formal divinity school came into being at Harvard, a resident graduate was one who stayed on after graduating from Harvard College in order to read for the ministry. One hundred years ago, a resident graduate at Harvard meant one who came from another divinity school, read in theology for a time, and then was graduated with the senior class of ministers. Today, it refers to a special student at the doctoral level without official program. My placement was in Applied Theology and the History of Religions, which is the closest Harvard could come to my real focus, psychology of religion and Asian studies.

My association with the ideas of Emanuel Swedenborg occurred as a result of work in the unpublished manuscript collection of the American philosopher-psychologist William James. When I came from SMU to Harvard Divinity School, I brought the techniques of historical scholarship from comparative religions, which, once at Harvard, I applied to archival investigation in the history of American psychology and psychiatry. This was a little unusual, since historical analysis in psychology is traditionally applied from the history of science, the history of medicine, or the more general history of Western civilization, but almost never from the history of religions, let alone the history of comparative religions.

From this vantage point, however, I was able to establish a stewardship over a number of scattered and previously abandoned library collections related primarily to James's works, but studying as well the works of other late-nineteenth-to-mid-twentieth-century Harvard physicians and psychologists, most of whom were interested in personality and consciousness, psychotherapy, or religious experience. These included, among others, the papers of Gordon Willard Allport, Henry A. Murray, Richard C. Cabot, James J. Putnam, and Stanley Cobb. The quip at the divinity school was that, using history, I soon became so successful at raising the dead (in religion) that I was asked to go over into medicine and try there (thought to be much more difficult).

My studies actually took me in two separate directions. First, after leaving the divinity school, I joined the faculty of Medicine at Harvard and became the historian in the Department of Psychiatry at the Massachusetts General Hospital, a position I have held for the past sixteen years. From that vantage point, I have continued to contribute to the scholarly literature on the history of academic psychology and psychiatry in the United States and more recently to the field of mind-body medicine.[4]

Second, my work in William James's unpublished manuscript collection led me to the archives of the Swedenborg School of Religion, where I found the James's family trunk containing a collection of books on Swedenborg owned by the family patriarch, Henry James, Sr. The trunk also contained extensive new documentation on the James's family relationship to Ralph Waldo Emerson and the Concord transcendentalists, dating from the 1840s to the 1880s, and the Swedenborgian roots of American pragmatism.

Swedenborgianism, for those who are unfamiliar with it, refers to a Christian denomination that follows the biblical interpretation of Emanuel Swedenborg, an eighteenth century scientist and interpreter of religious experience. It can also refer more generally to avid readers of Swedenborg's works, such as the New England transcendentalists, who were not members of the religious movement, but who used Swedenborg's ideas to corroborate their own interior journey toward self-realization.[5] Henry James, Sr., father of both William and his younger brother Henry, the novelist, wrote numerous works on Swedenborg and was a main conduit for Swedenborgian ideas found in Emerson and others. Emerson and James, Sr., were close friends; indeed, Emerson was William James's godfather. Later, as they matured into their separate vocations, William and Henry, Jr., became heirs to the Swedenborgian and transcendentalist literary legacy, which is, at its base, an intuitive psychology of character formation. The two brothers then transmuted this literary legacy, one into science, the other into literature.

At the same time, although not widely acknowledged today, Swedenborgian ideas had a major impact on American popular psychology in the nineteenth century, where the avenues of Swedenborgian influence often paralleled that of New England transcendentalism.[6] It is precisely at this juncture that my interpretations of Swedenborg part company with catachists of the Church of the New Jerusalem, as their interpretation of Swedenborg is primarily theological and christological, while mine is preeminently psychological, taken as an interior language of personality transformation. As such, in my interpretation of Swedenborg, I am probably closer to Emersonian transcendentalism, or even the modern works of authors such as Wilson van Dusen, than I am to many contemporary New Church men and women.[7]

Nevertheless, my twenty-year excursion into Swedenborg and his influence on American culture and into transcendentalism and its milieu has also taken me into documenting the history of American folk psychology, a psychospiritual tradition of interior experience that has been around since the founding of the American colonies and that continues to assert its influence today in the New Age movement, counterculture psychotherapy, or alternative religions. Collectively, I refer to the history of this popular spiritual psychology as the American visionary tradition.[8]

These various lines of investigation have led me inexorably to the present statement, which I envision primarily as a book about consciousness and healing. Traditionally, physicians have busied themselves with talking about healing from a scientific point of view, while theologians have discussed healing from the standpoint of creeds and denominational beliefs. Meanwhile, psychoanalysts have written extensively about consciousness and mental health, but they have done so from a strictly Freudian point of view.

Now, however, a new generation of practitioners in alternative therapy and complementary medicine discusses healing in the context of holistic health or mind-body medicine. Larry Dossey and Bernie Siegel are two well-known examples of these new voices. There is also an extensive popular literature on consciousness from the standpoint of humanistic and transpersonal psychology, based originally on the work of Carl Rogers, Abraham Maslow, and Rollo May, and now following authors such as Stanley Krippner, Robert Ornstein, Stanislav Grof, Jeanne Achterberg, Joan Borysenko, and others.

As a further complement to these voices, I offer this text on consciousness and healing from a psychological point of view by a historian and philosopher of psychology with a background in Asian studies. I propose that there is an important piece missing from our contemporary definitions of health and wellness, namely, a dynamic psychology of immediate experience that each of us constructs for ourselves as a way to make sense out of reality.

Such a psychology, according to numerous interpreters besides myself, can be found embedded in the writings of Emanuel Swedenborg. Helen Keller, an ardent reader of Swedenborg, wrote a book about his influence in her life, entitled *My Religion*.[9] William Blake was heavily influenced by Swedenborg's writings. Honoré Balzac incorporated Swedenborg's ideas in his novels. The nineteenth-century landscape painter George Inness developed an internal geometry of form and color based on Swedenborgian thought. Swedenborgian ideas influenced the art of Hiram Powers, Howard Pyle, and William Page. Ralph Waldo Emerson even devoted a chapter to Swedenborg in *Representative Men* (1850), claiming Swedenborg as an example of a man who looked within and showed how to contact divinity directly, independent of denominational churches, scriptural texts, and a priesthood.

Swedenborg's writings provided a popular language of interior experience that reached millions of readers through interpreters such as the spiritualist-divine Andrew Jackson Davis; Warren Felt Evans, the founder of the New Thought Movement (himself a Swedenborgian minister); Unitarian and Congregationalist ministers such as Thomas Lake Harris; and transcendentalists such as Emerson and Henry James, Sr. According to Henry Ward Beecher, no one could know the theology of the nineteenth-century America who had not read Swedenborg's writings. Of course, Sigmund Freud also provided a language of interior experience that was popular throughout the twentieth century, although in the American psychotherapeutic counterculture today, the writings of the Swiss psychiatrist C. G. Jung are considered somewhat more relevant.

The search is still on, however, for a psychology adequate to the psychospiritual needs of contemporary individuals whose interior experiences have far exceeded anything that institutional science and organized religion can adequately describe. The direction this search has taken is now into the domain of healing. For in modern culture today, it is not sufficient simply to understand spiritual experiences. What we now require is a definitive sign of their practical effects.

A Psychology of Spiritual Healing 2

Consciousness and Healing

What is a psychology of spiritual healing? Here we have a complex question that is susceptible to several different angles of interpretation. To tease out a workable answer, we might first ask what is meant by psychology in this context.

First of all, this is not a psychology in the usual academic sense of the term. It does not rely on studies in animal learning, theories of sexual pathology, or the computer modeling of cognitive thought processes. Rather, it is a psychology that is at once experiential, existential, and projective—a psychology that, in all likelihood, is the primary vehicle through which not only self-healing but also personal growth and spiritual transformation take place. It is my conclusion that studying this psychology as a process of inner exploration within individual lives and across cultures suggests that there is an important and heretofore overlooked relationship yet to be clarified between consciousness and healing.

The problem is that such a language of interior experience has no credibility in modern culture except if you are a poet, a songwriter, or a storyteller; or perhaps a psychotherapist or pastoral counselor; or a mother singing her baby to sleep each night. It is not generally the language of everyday discourse because it is so personal. It is not the kind of language that drives science or business, and it is not normally the speech we hear when talking to our neighbors, although it sometimes appears in the language of relationships, such as between intimate friends, or in the expression of romantic feelings. It is, rather, a deeply interior language. There are, however, some indications of it in outward culture.

I am reminded of the late Dr. Mark Altschule of Harvard University, whose joke on the founding of psychotherapy was that a Greek poet once hung out a sign that read "In need of new material. Come in and tell me your troubles." Similarly, playrights and novelists have long used the device of the interior monologue to reveal characters or to build plot. Indeed, the development of the psychological novel in the twentieth century was represented by a shift away from a simple succession of outward events to page after page of what the protagonist was thinking and feeling.

The type of interior psychology I am describing is not just an everyday interior monologue, however, although that is a beginning. A psychology adequate to understand spiritual experience is, first of all, experiential; it begins in the here-and-now. It recognizes that everything comes to us in the immediate moment. It recognizes that all memories are reconstructions of the past in our present state of consciousness and that all thoughts of the future are projections from the present, mere probablility statements about what might happen. No matter what the memory or forecast, it is generated in the here-and-now, the focal point through which all experience comes to us in whatever form.

This also means that such a psychology is idiosyncratic. It is solitary, in the sense that it is forged by the individual alone, even though it may find corroboration from the experience of others. It is unique in that it is exactly like no other, although, by and large, it suffers from the same universal limitations of language, time, and circumstance imposed upon everyone who tries to construct for him or herself a system for understanding reality out of language.

Most importantly, such a psychology is psychodynamic. It recognizes that the awareness of the present moment—our present, everyday state of consciousness—is at any time surrounded by deeper layers of the unconscious, which remain out of sight but which, nevertheless, exert a powerful influence on our every thought, word, and deed. It recognizes that psychic energy, the spirit of consciousness that is the unique person, takes on various forms, and that the form the energy of one state takes must be converted into a different form for expression in another state. The meaning hidden behind a thought we have in the waking state, for instance, might only be revealed in dream imagery. This is to say that the energy of the unconscious can only be expressed to consciousness in the indirect form of the dream, while the conscious thought is the sanitized version of what the unconscious is really trying to tell us. The word "dynamic," therefore, refers to the transformation of energy from one state of consciousness to another.

A psychology sufficient to comprehend spiritual experience is also visionary, meaning that the contents of the unconscious are expressed to consciousness in the form of symbols that must be interpreted to be understood. While there are metaphors, similes, and imagery that express the general energy of the unconscious, the inward journey toward self-realization involves the search for deep symbols that reflect the person's singular destiny. The deeper one fathoms, in fact, the greater the probablility that imagery will emerge that might sound to others as apocalyptic or mythic in character.

Such a psychology is also growth-oriented; that is, it points towards the transcendent. It should inspire moral and aesthetic ends; it should encourage the individual to reach for what is highest and best; and it should also be programmatic, offering a blueprint for actualizing something more than what presently can be conceived, so that it is grounded in the idea that transforming the present fragmented state into something more whole is always possible.

That being so, such a psychology must also be able to express generically what is existential, or ultimate, in a person's life. The highest experience or the farthest state that the person has ever encountered must find representation in some form (as well as the lowest, with which we are all too familiar), whether artistic, linguistic, or physical. Such representations of the ultimate I have referred to as the iconography of the transcendent, meaning symbolic representation of the highest possible state of consciousness the person has experienced in whatever form that might take.

Finally, such a psychology is predicated on an opening of the internal doors of perception. There must be a movement beyond the confines of waking consciousness. There must be an opening into deeper and richer realms of internal experience. There must be an experience of something beyond the finite person, something more than the product of mere intellect, something beyond the bounds of material reality. Such experiences occur to people all the time. This woman may have been born with such an internal sense. That man may have experienced such an opening because of a traumatic experience as a child. That group over there may have witnessed a collective vision that it had earnestly sought as the result of some communion; this group over here may have experienced it as the result of completing some gargantuan task together, whether survival of a harrowing experience or the achievement of some great social aim.

I take as my starting point what is typically meant by consciousness, since it is here, within our present consciousness, that we recognize that healing of any kind has taken place. In this endeavor, I will borrow a few pages from William James.[1]

To be conscious, is, first of all, to be aware. Consciousness seems to be what we know and remember. It is the space in which we live that we call our own, or at least the one within which we move, breathe, and have our being. To be conscious in this sense means not only to recognize that we are aware, but to recognize that there are fluctuations in our level of awareness. Some days we are very sensitive; other days we are completely insensitive. Some days we remember things; other days we are completely forgetful. All of this happens within our awareness. When we are not aware, most of us presume that we are not conscious. Thus, consciousness seems to expand and contract.

Sleep we take as a state of unconsciousness, as in a coma or stupor. Our mothers had to wake us up when we were young by calling our names several times until we recognized what was happening. At that point, we woke up; only then did we became conscious. Trauma teams in the ambulance unit typically keep asking the patient, "Do you know your name?" and "Can you remember where you are?" because such recognition is a sign of being and remaining conscious. So, to be aware also means to associate consciousness with our personal identity.

The second thing we believe about our consciousness is that it flows. It is constantly changing. It moves inexorably onward. The present is always in motion, quickly becoming the past as it rushes into the future. In this sense, we experience consciousness as a stream. It is a river into which we never step in the same place twice. A thought had twice over is always a new thought the second time around because a memory is some remnant of the past re-experienced in the present. Meanwhile, the immediate panorama also constantly changes. Events unfold before us; we observe that living things are born, mature, and decay. Everything appears in a state of construction and deconstruction, evolution and dissolution. So too with the drama that unfolds before the footlights of our field of waking awareness. Thoughts succeed each other. Words come out in sequences, and objects change color; and as the bright of day is succeeded by the dark of night, so too we are awake for a time and then we sleep—a total of some twenty-two years spent asleep for a seventy-year-old person. In and out of awareness we go, day and night, in a continuing cycle.

Nevertheless, another fact about consciousness is that, despite the constant change, there always seems to be something sensibly continuous about it. Almost all of the cells in my body have become completely transformed, sloughed off and renewed, thousands of times since I was born; yet, to me, I remain the same person through all these changes. When I go to sleep at night, I awaken the next morning in the same body. I do not suddenly wake up as someone else, nor do I awaken and feel that who I was before is now a stranger to my present self. Rather, I am keenly aware of the constancy of my identity from moment to moment, from hour to hour, and day to day.

And yet a fourth characteristic of my present consciousness is that there appears to be a radical difference between the "I" and the "not-I," between me as I feel and experience reality and reality that seems to be outside myself. Consciousness, in other words, always seems to deal with objects as if they were independent of itself. The entire world seems to be made up of things other than myself. The world "out there" seems to be filled with objects and people, while the world inside my head seems to be filled with ideas, images, and memories—in other words, with representations of all those objects in the world. So, we believe that reality is always counted twice, once out there and once inside our brains.

Finally, consciousness is selective. Out of the great blooming, buzzing confusion, consciousness selects certain parts and ignores the rest. I pay attention to what I am interested in; all else is a blur, unattended to, unnoticed. I see what I am trained by habit to notice. I am more likely to miss what is novel because I am too busy attending to what I already know. Instead, I embrace the familiar, largely because it is already my own.

So, consciousness appears to be personal; ever-changing, yet continuous; independent of objects and selective about what it perceives. This, of course, is not all. Other definitions posit the existence of hidden unconscious forces, and point to the reality of other possible states of awareness from the pathological to the transcendent. But for now, we will confine ourselves to a definition of consciousness as personal identity, that condition of our everyday existence with which we are most familiar.

This brings us, of course, to the problem of personal identity. Who or what is the self that is healed? Unabashedly, William James offers the interpretation that we are, in fact, many selves at once.

There is, first of all, James says, the biological self. In this mode, we are our physical bodies, our physiological processes; we are these tissues, these organs, these genes that appear before us. We are defined by the date of our birth, the color of our eyes, our finger- and footprints, the unique pattern of our irises, just this heart, just these lungs, just these genes. Let anything happen to any one of them and we are no longer the complete self we were before. This is the biological self, the history of my diseases, the story of how I got this scar and this bruise—in short, the biological me.

There is also the material self. In this mode, we define ourselves as all the objects that we own. I am this house, that car, these clothes, that school I attend, that job I perform. I have a personal relationship with each object such that it is not only mine, but that it is actually an extension of me. I took it personally the last time I had to throw out an old pair of favorite shoes. We had been together a long time, we had gone many places together, so many things had happened to us. They were so comfortable; it seemed as if I was just breaking them in when they finally fell apart. They and I were one. I lingered for a nostalgic moment over the trash can where I threw them, but then walked off in my new pair of shined black leather dress shoes, at which time my love affair with some other aspect of the world of objects began all over again.

There is also the social self. In fact, there is a different self for each relationship that we have, James said. To each person we show a different side, so that we are never the same in each relationship; and with each person we also adapt, so that new sides of our self may also emerge. We are to every other individual some conjunction of how we wish them to see us and their own projections of who they think we are. And in this way no two relationships are alike, nor is each self of our many selves.

Then there is the empirical "I," the "I" that is the subject of every sentence about myself; the sum total of my biological, material, and social selves; the pronoun to which all that is known by or about me refers. The empirical "I," however, stands in stark contrast to the spiritual self, that part of me known only to myself.

The spiritual self is the interior "I" beyond my thoughts and feelings, beyond the memories of what I have owned, what I have done, and whom I have known. This is the unfathomable part of my personality that is so extraordinarily famliar on the one hand and yet so elusive on the other, since it is beyond words, beyond labels, beyond conceptualization. Yet it is intimately who I really am.

❧ The Doorway to the Spiritual Self ❦

Here we have arrived at the threshold of the unknown, at the portal through which only the individual can go, at this last juncture between the domain of publically shared knowledge and the privacy of the interior self. Here our discussion of healing should begin, because it is here that a psychology of inner experience is forged. This is the point where the subjective and the objective meet, where opposites meld into one experience, where everything experienced takes place—the immediate moment. At this point, I propose to have a different look at what we traditionally mean by healing.

Physical healing in Western medicine is typically thought of as what the doctor does; what science tells us is the nature of reality; what medications can be synthesized, tested, and massed produced. Meanwhile, healing of the spirit is confined to the discussions of theologians or to accounts in popular nonfiction, where it most often falls under the catagory of religion. Children see the Virgin Mary and afterwards throngs come to be healed at that same site. A charismatic priest puts his hand over a set of crippled legs and immediately the person rises and walks. A terminal cancer patient sees a vision of God and the tumors disappear. This is the great divide in modern culture: science versus religion, both competing to co-opt the other and remain standing as the reigning definition of reality. Is the universe made up solely of atoms and molecules, a vast vacuum of space, to be explained only in scientific terms? Or is the universe the creation of an omnipotent, omniscient, and omnipresent God, in which he is the ultimate explanation of what is? We cannot even conceive that there might be a third alternative. Our tendency has been to polarize just these two great systems of thought and to keep them radically separate. The American constitution guarantees the separation of church and state, while the state is free to pour millions of dollars into science. Meanwhile, there are also factions attempting to Christianize science, in which scientific evidence is put forward to prove events in the Bible, or the principles of physics are invoked to ratify Christian doctrine. Organized science, however, has continued to resist the advances of organized religion.

While science and religion remain separate as cultural institutions, there have been increasingly successful attempts to measure spirit. If individuals practice the Relaxation Response, pioneered by cardiologist Herbert Benson, a simple technique for achieving deep body rest, while repeating sacred teachings from their religion, tests show that headaches disappear, premenstrual symptoms abate, blood pressure goes down, dosage of medications can sometimes be cut, and so forth. As the physician Larry Dossey has amply demonstrated, there is suggestive evidence for the positive influence of prayer at a distance.[2] Groups of patients who receive prayers from others at a distance got better sooner, as opposed to comparable groups of patients who received no such ministrations. Other researchers have shown that breast cancer patients who attend support groups tend to live longer than others who remain solitary, heart patients who go on a low-fat diet and meditate can reverse cholesterol buildup; psoriasis patients receiving both standard light treatment and positive guided mental imagery have seen their skin clear faster than those who have received just the light treatment, and so on. Evidence is mounting that, under the proper circumstances, when we couple physical interventions with psychospiritually oriented ones, conditions are created to find positive, measurable differences in health and wellness. In fact, there has been so much activity in this area lately that it is now identified as a distinct field under various names such as holistic health, energy medicine, mind-body medicine, or complementary therapy.[3]

Unfortunately, an examination of even this new area of medical science shows that, while consciousness and healing seem to be the topics under discussion, the information explosion is still all about symptoms, remedies, and methods of appraisal. Healing is discussed; but there is, as yet, no systematic understanding of consciousness, no discussion of any kind of psychology more sophisticated than a layman's knowledge of Freud and Jung, and no psychology that is sufficiently projective, visionary, or mythic, although there has been definite movement in that direction from transpersonal psychologists who have borrowed heavily from theosophy or the Asian religious traditions of Hinduism, Buddhism, or Taoism.

The Relationship between Consciousness and Healing

Throughout the history of the world's religious traditions, especially those that have developed a sophisticated inward study of consciousness, spiritual experience has been associated with healing in all its forms.

In his work *Shamanism: Archaic Techniques of Ecstasy*, the comparative religionist Mircea Eliade has written about Siberian shamanism and the cultivation of trance states for purposes of divination and curing. Mythologist Jospeh Campbell in his classic work *Hero with a Thousand Faces* extracted the generic and prototypical motifs from a variety of shamanic cultures, outlining the mythic cycle of the hero's quest, his inward journey, and subsequent return as a transformed being, who then takes up the role of healer in primitive society. Meanwhile, in *Discovery of the Unconscious*, psychiatrist and historian Henri Ellenberger has counted the shamanic cycle as a starting point for understanding contemporary developments in dynamic psychotherapy. Shamanism, in fact, has become the new vogue in counterculture psychotherapy.[1]

As I understand the shamanic experience, the shaman, first of all, has been trained to enter into trance states at will, or at least when the conditions are right for such entry. When patients come to a shaman, an inquiry is made into the presenting complaint; but the shaman, like the scientifically trained physician, also looks for any outward signs of distress that will indicate more about the patient. The healer will also look within him- or herself and take a reading on what might be felt intuitively or seen clairvoyantly. The patients, of course, come with certain expectations, so to an extent, they display their stories and problems for all who are developed enough to interpret their manner, voice, and physical appearance.

The shaman, through a variety of means, then begins a process of altering his or her own consciousness. Patients either participate in this alteration and, through a rapport that has been established, travel through their own consciousness with the shaman, or else remain behind while the healer travels to an inaccessible state of consciousness that might contain pertinent information—in the form of a song, a dance, an herb, or an idea related to the illness or the cure. The shaman may have taken this journey innumerable times or may travel to a space never before visited. To get there, the healer may transform his physical body into that of an animal; he may fly or fall or arrive by otherwise occult means. Events of import for the sick person may occur on the way. Beings may be encountered that create obstacles to be overcome. Internal battles may be fought to reach the secret that will heal the patient. Sometimes, the return might be thwarted, preventing the safe delivery of whatever is meant to be brought back. In shamanic cultures, trance states of this kind play a key role in the healing process.

In the villages of north India, the local healer is called the *tabib*, if a Muslim, or *ved*, if a Hindu. While the *ved* may have extensive experience dealing with sick people, he draws from a long line of medicinal teachings from the Vedas, the four great books of early Brahmanic Hinduism. The Upanishads, the highest philosophical teachings of the Vedas, present the philosophy and psychology of consciousness underlying the formulas in the medicinal texts.[5] The teachings of the Vedas recognize the state of waking, the state of sleep with dreams, the state of deep, profound sleep without dreams, and the state of superconsciousness, the essence of that which is at one with the Supreme Self. These states are employed differentially for healing.

Tibetan medicine, which draws from the healing traditions of both Vedic Hinduism and traditional Chinese Taoism, as well as its own indigenous sources, prescribes both herbal remedies and meditation exercises, along with psychosocial prescriptions with each diagnosis of a patient's illness. Both psychological and physical techniques of healing are integral with the spiritual teachings of Tibetan Buddhism. Psychology is not a separate category of Tibetan medicine, but an integral part of each diagnosis.[6]

There is also a close association between states of altered consciousness and healing in cultures of hunter-gatherers. Richard Katz in his work *Boiling Energy* has provided extensive field study of the Kung in the Kalahari Desert of South Africa that shows the communal trance-dance to be the center of village life as well as the source of solutions for physical and mental ailments of tribal members.[7] Villagers, healers, and the afflicted dance together all night long in a continuous circle around a fire to generate the *num*, or heat. *Num* is spiritual energy shared by everyone, although the dance rituals are frequently performed for the sole benefit of a sick tribal member. In this way, everyone partakes of the healing energy.

Similarly, the training of doctors in the Yurok Indian tribe of northern California involved the induction of altered states in a sweat lodge.[8] Women, the traditional healers of this tribe, would enter a sweat lodge and, on entering a trance state, would dance until they felt pains in certain parts of their bodies. They would continue until they had danced the pain away, so that from that point on, they were known as the doctor of that particular pain in that part of the body. With their newfound ability, they could take away the same pain of others, because they knew how to seek out and endure the pain in themselves.

Western audiences are familiar with the New Testament stories of healings performed by Jesus. While there are scattered references in the Old Testament to miraculous healings and resurrection of the dead, most examples are found in the New Testament Gospels, which chiefly describe the healing ministry of Jesus. Jesus was said to have cured fevers and healed lepers, to have caused the blind to see and the lame to walk, to have called men, women, and children back from the dead, and to have cast out demons. He performed his miracles on individuals or on groups. He dealt with whomever was brought to him, but he also sought out people to heal. In all cases, the healings were performed to transform the consciousness of the sick by faith, not simply to restore health to their bodies. If they did not necessarily believe in Christ's power before they were healed, the Bible tells us that they certainly did after.

An important interpretation clearly linking outward healing to the internal language of consciousness was put forth by Emanuel Swedenborg. Swedenborg believed that he had received a dispensation from God, communicated to him through the angels, to interpret the internal spiritual meaning of the Bible. By this, Swedenborg understood that the words of the Bible were symbols pointing not to physical or historical events in the material world but to insights about the spiritual transformation of consciousness. All outward events were, therefore, subject to an internal spiritual interpretation.

If we apply Swedenborg's method, we can see that the underlying purpose of the physical healings performed by Jesus was to open up the cured and their witnesses (and, by extension, all who read or hear the story) to the wider interior domain of spiritual consciousness that most people do not see in the normal waking state. When the man who was blind from birth came to Jesus, Jesus spat on the ground, mixed the earth into clay with his spittle, and anointed the man's eyes with the mixture. He then told the man to go and wash in a certain body of water; when the man did this, his sight came to him for the first time. From this episode, the man not only gained his physical sight, but, analyzing the internal meaning, became a witness to the vision of internal spiritual life.

In all these instances, healing and consciousness are connected. It is a curious phenomenon of modern Western culture that, after the divorce of science from religion and the marriage of medicine with science, consciousness and healing have become radically separate, and methods of physical healing have been elevated, while the spiritual dimension of healing has been all but eliminated from social discussion until only recently. A very old idea, which is central to our present discussion, but perhaps a novel one to modern readers, is that consciousness and healing are, in fact, linked and that this connection can best be understood within the context of a growth-oriented psychology of self-realization.

The Meaning of
Suffering

ealing begins with the consecration of the affections. This involves a transformation in our current state of waking, mundane consciousness, where analytic thought is set aside and we transform our emotions from merely pleasurable and painful attachment to objects in the external world into higher levels of spiritual feeling. In physical illness, we may be able to transform self-pity into gratitude for our caregivers or into concern for someone less fortunate than ourselves; pain can be endured if we learn to invoke a higher purpose. As every surgeon has witnessed, even a positive attitude about the outcome of a major operation can lead to a speedy, even miraculous recovery, while negativity and pessimism on the patient's part is often accompanied by complications such as lowered resistance to infection, more frequent complaints, and poorer outcomes.

Similarly, in a spiritual sense, earthy love can be transformed into heavenly compassion; feelings for or against a person or group can become transformed into equanimity. In this way, emotions become vehicles to spiritual progress, instead of obstacles.

Take, for instance, the transformation of suffering. This was the topic taught by the Venerable Lama Anagarika Govinda, a German-born Theravada monk who had studied the Vajrayana tradition of Tibet.[1] Govinda came to Perkins School of Theology in the spring of 1973 when I was in my final semester, where he taught a course on the historical and spiritual development of Buddhism. It was an extraordinary experience for several reasons.

First, Perkins School of Theology is a conservative Methodist institution devoted to preparing pulpit preachers in various forms of missionary Christianity, and this was the first time that an ordained Buddhist monk had been invited to teach a course that was open to the entire theological school and to students of Southern Methodist University, the college affiliated with the divinity school. Govinda's presence set the stage for the possibility of a unique dialogue between local Christian theologians who would not normally come into contact with devotees of non-Western religions and those scholars and practitioners of Buddhism who had assembled around Govinda for the year he was there.

Second, Govinda was a Western translator of an Eastern tradition, one who had mastered the requisite textual languages of Pali and Sanskrit and who had become advanced enough in the practice of Buddhist meditation to be recognized as an adept by the Buddhists themselves. As such, he was uniquely suited to interpret the message of Buddhism to Western audiences

Third, Govinda's visit was also important because Buddhism is primarily a non-theistic religion and he spoke about a spiritual psychology that focused on an alteration of one's own state of consciousness as the primary vehicle for alleviating human suffering. While this change in state of consciousness is achieved through meditation, meditation in Buddhism actually means something quite different than similar-sounding techniques referred to in Western contemplative traditions. Christianity, on the other hand, emphasizes prayer and the relationship between the individual and a higher power.

Despite these differences, Govinda spoke directly to the experience of his audience by creating an atmosphere of transformation that seemed to pervade the lecture hall. Some understood his subject from an intellectual standpoint, but some also were involved in similar forms of personal practice. Meanwhile, others came to be healed, not to learn about the technical aspects of Buddhism, but to receive what the Hindus call *darshan*, to hear the teachings and be in the presence of someone who had dedicated his life to Buddhism. With *darshan*, simply to be present when the teachings are transmitted is to be healed.

Suffering and the means to overcome it were the central themes of Govinda's message about Buddhism. The Buddhist view is that no human being escapes from suffering. The classic Theravada texts emphasize this point with the story of a mother who approached the Buddha and his disciples. The mother implored the Buddha, whom she believed to be an enlightened being, to take away the pain and agony she was then experiencing from the death of her beloved son. She asked over and over again, would the Buddha please take away her pain. The Buddha responded that, before her pain could be taken away, she would have to perform one task: she would have to go from door to door throughout the city until she had located just one person who had not suffered from the loss of a loved one.

The woman hurried away and several days later came back a changed person. She had not succeeded in her mission; she was not able to locate a single person whose life had been free from the sorrow accompanying the loss of a loved one. In fact, the more doors she knocked on, the more stories she heard of woe and despair. Finally, she realized a basic psychological law of human nature. Not only is no one free from suffering, but most people are in the same state as herself. With the realization that she was not alone, her pain eased.

The lesson here, of course, is that we take our own experience of suffering as unique, solely as our own. In the midst of it, no one could possibly know how bad we feel. Since no one could have the same experience, it is only a short step to conclude that no one has suffered as we have. Upon deeper inquiry, however, we find as the woman did that no one, rich or poor, educated or ignorant, escapes the sting of sickness and death. Everyone has a grievous tale to tell about the loss of a loved one. Here, it is the loss of a baby; there, it is a companion of fifty or sixty years; and, over there, it is the death of a mother or father. The specific details always differ, but in the larger frame of things, all are equal in this experience.

The other important lesson from this story is one of self-realization. The woman's suffering was lifted when she realized that she was not alone and isolated. We can imagine her going from door to door, listening to the suffering of others, and out of her eventual understanding, ministering to their needs. To hear others tell of their sorrows not only carries us outside ourselves into

the wider realm of human relationships, but also trans-
mutes our feelings from the level of self-centeredness
to the more universal experience of equanimity and
compassion.

This account of the woman from a Buddhist's perspective suggested to Govinda's theological audience
that there are many analogies within Christian theology
to the universality of suffering. I concluded that the most
emblematic is the crucifixion and resurrection of Jesus.
The passion of the cross is depicted in every Catholic
church as the fourteen stations of Jesus on his way to
Calvary, and reenacted through the streets of Jerusalem
by devout Christians every year on Good Friday. On a
pilgrimage one time to all the old cathedrals throughout
the French city of Nantes, I had a chance to study different artistic renditions of the fourteen stations. In this
often-repeated sequence, Jesus is betrayed by one of his
own, tried and convicted, publicly humiliated by having
to carry his own cross through the city, and then slowly
crucified. The final station is the entombment. Traditionally, there has been no visual representation of the
resurrection. The emphasis is all on the suffering of the
crucifixion. One sees this emphasis plainly on the face of
the wooden carvings of Jesus on the altars of the California missions, executed in such fine but graphic detail by
American Indians indoctrinated into Catholicism.

While this emphasis on the crucifixion has been a
principal criticism of Catholicism, Catholics point out
that the suffering of Jesus is depicted to teach gratitude
that Jesus gave his life for the forgiveness of our sins.
Thus, to the extent that we can emotionally empathize
with his extreme suffering, we can understand the measure of the sacrifice that someone else has made on our
behalf. Numerous other moral consequences then follow. Forgiveness of others and self-sacrifice in the name

of higher principles are but two of the virtues that might be learned from the contemplation of Jesus' suffering.

One does not have to be a Catholic to appreciate the spiritual significance of suffering particularly depicted by this motif. While I am not a Catholic, I do have a very large crucifix on the wall of my home in remembrance of an incident from my early youth in which, for the first time, I experienced the awakening of a religious emotion around the experience of suffering.

The occasion was a typical domestic situation in a middle-class American household. I was about seven years old at the time and, still in the throes of boyhood terrors, wanted to have one of my parents come back after I had been tucked in bed for the night and after the lights had been turned out. I remember that my first ploy had been to call out to my mother and father, who were on the other side of the apartment, separated from me by closed doors. My mother actually came in for a moment. She did not stay but, just poking her head in, assured me that everything was all right and that I would fall asleep soon. Not satisfied, I remember calling out again a few times, but to no avail.

I remember thinking that if they heard me crying, one of them would surely come in and stay with me for a longer period. The problem was that I could not just voluntarily bring on the tears. It occurred to me to think of something that would make me sad, hoping that it would be sad enough to cry over. Unsuccessfully, I tried thinking of one or two things; but then, spontaneously, I fixed on the image of the crucifixion. The longer I visualized that limp body, hanging there, bleeding from nails that had been driven into the hands and feet, gouged in the side by a spear from the mocking guards, forehead dripping with blood from the crown of thorns, the more I felt repulsed and sickened. I tried to remember why this act had been perpetrated against someone; I began to feel resentment, and a great sense of injustice came over me. I also began to feel frustrated because there was nothing I could do to help the figure in my image from his obviously painful circumstances.

At this point, a rather remarkable change began to take place in me. I did indeed begin to cry, but it was a silent weeping that I found to my amazement I did not want anyone else to hear. This was accompanied by a distinct visual change in the atmosphere around my bed, in which the entire area became filled with a soft but low-toned light. I remember seeing a crucified figure above and behind me as I lay in my bed, as if the figure had somehow become fused with the headboard. As I emitted low, quiet sobs, I felt a great sympathy with this figure, and I remember distinctly that I felt a heroic feeling of self-sacrifice. The explanation I recalled from Sunday school was that this event had happened for some higher spiritual purpose. It was a purpose, however, which I did not fully understand. Afterwards, I fell off immediately into sleep.

I have held that vision before me for almost fifty years now and can see it as vividly as that first night. I do not associate it with Catholicism or with the teachings of any Christian denomination, but rather see it as a benchmark experience in my own inward spiritual development. Subsequently, about twenty years later, while traveling to get to my parents' somewhat out-of-the-way place, I stopped at an old antique store. In the back, behind a lot of piled furniture, tossed over on its side, was a wooden crucifix that reminded me of my vision. The shop owner said it had come from a Methodist church nearby that had closed, and in the year or two it had been in his shop, no one had taken an interest in it. It needed some repair, so he sold it to me for a few dollars.

I took it home, mended it, and hung it on my wall as a way to keep my external attention focused on my internal vision.

Recently, while working on what I have called a history of the American visionary tradition, I read that the charismatic evangelical preacher Frank Buchman, founder of the Oxford group, had experienced a similar vision in 1914, while attending a lecture on the resurrection.[2] There, Buchman had a vision of the crucifixion and afterwards was moved to found the Oxford Group, which soon became a worldwide spiritual organization, later known as Moral Re-Armament. Its major offshoot in the 1930s became Alcoholics Anonymous, prototype of the twelve-step programs of the American self-help movement.

The other side of Jesus' suffering, then, is the resurrection, one of the pivotal beliefs of Christianity. Belief in this event represents the great dividing line between the Old and the New Testament. While there is a large theological literature on the resurrection, in Catholicism it has always been considered the first of the "Five Glorious Mysteries." Indeed, as my trip through the cathedrals at Nantes had shown me, the fourteen stations of the cross have traditionally ended with the entombment. Now, with a new catechism, however, churches are permitted the option to add to the fourteen stations of the cross a fifteenth, which depicts Jesus' rising from the dead.

Carl Jung pointed out the manner in which, in the West, belief in the resurrection has become transformed into a secular goal of consciousness.[3] Psychologically, we have separated science from religion but have transmuted the spiritual idea of the resurrection into a secular psychology of character development. In this sphere of psychological consciousness, therapeutic healing is believed to take place. Transcendence, the experience of going from the lesser state of suffering to the higher state of grace, has now become equated with progress. We do things in order to become better persons: we diet, we work hard and invest, we acquire knowledge that changes us. Everywhere about us we are encouraged to better ourselves. In secular terms, for Jung, these injunctions represent the secularization of a Christian, particularly a Protestant, idea.

Another common example of transmuting a religious idea into a secular one is the confession. In modern terms, the confession of the church has been secularized into one of the primary techniques of psychotherapy. We reveal secrets hidden in the unconscious to our therapist and relive on the couch past emotional traumas, sometimes long forgotten. We reintegrate these experiences back into waking consciousness as part of our recovery. The kind of insight that takes place in psychotherapy performs a function similar to the sacrament of confession and the remission of sins within the church. Even the goals of certain forms of therapy, such as those of Jung or of American transpersonal psychologists such as Stanislav Grof, are self-consciously defined in terms that make them psychotherapies of transcendence, their main purpose being to explore states of consciousness beyond that of the normal waking condition.[4] The patient is encouraged particularly to actualize states that, in the conceptual framework of the treatment, are considered more spiritual than the waking state, for it is in the experience of transcendence, transpersonal therapists believe, that we are truly healed.

A moving example of the psychotherapy of transcendence is Victor Frankl's logotherapy.[5] Frankl, a Viennese Jew and a physician trained as a psychoanalyst, survived the Nazi concentration camps during World

War II. In the camps, he saw suffering beyond human imagination, beyond anything that could be conceived by those who were not there. At the same time, however, he saw extraordinary acts of heroism, unexpected generosity, and the highest expressions of human feeling. In the face of death and pain as daily commonplace occurrences, events took place that he could only describe as spiritual. He saw that sometimes the most horrible circumstances provide the opportunity to reveal what is best and highest within us. Sometimes, it was only giving away a crust of bread that had been saved; sometimes, it was a greater sacrifice, as when a prisoner offered to substitute himself for another on the way to the gas chamber.

Frankl emerged from these experiences a changed man. There was much more to human experience than depicted in the theories of Freud that he had learned as a young Viennese psychiatrist. So, it was no wonder that, after his experiences in the concentration camps, he became an existentialist. He had gone beyond the known, faced the abyss of human experience, and returned to tell about it. He called his new therapy for healing logotheraphy. It was, he said, not a therapy of the mind or the body, but a therapy for the soul.

As he relates in his classic work *Man's Search for Meaning*, Frankl sees "meaning" as the highest human achievement. Most people seek happiness, but they never find it. Others look for pleasure or for the rewards of recognition or for material wealth. Nothing, however, surpasses meaning because, when we have meaning, we have a reason to live, even under the worst circumstances. When we have meaning, we have affirmation of our existence, no matter how terrible or how painful it is. When we have meaning, even happiness comes to us; it comes almost unbidden in the form of great satisfaction, but it comes as a blessing, because it is now a by-product, not the goal, of our thoughts and actions.

Frankl's experiences in the camps and his subsequent encounters with his patients showed him that meaning comes to us in two ways. The first way is through suffering. Intractable pain, unending sorrow, constant torment of any kind always set us to asking why this or that has happened to us. We try to extract some lesson out of our circumstances. If we cannot, we give up, because we have no reason to go on. But it is a particular quality of the human spirit that we can find in the most insignificant image a sense of hope and the strength to endure what has beset us. Sometimes, to invent meaning where there is none can become a reason to live, because it can be the deciding factor between who lives and who dies. Surely, the one with hope rather than the one without is the one who tips the scales in favor of life, especially where human will and endurance are concerned.

But, Frankl says, meaning can also come to us through the actualization of values. All of us have ideals and goals to strive for, images of what we want to achieve or become, quests on which we have embarked, or loyalties we have made to cherished causes. Making these come about by our own efforts constitutes one of the highest experiences of human beings. It may be a young athlete's winning the Olympic gold medal; it may be a middle-aged mother's finishing college. It may be the first step on the moon; it may be the first step after a terrible car crash. These kinds of experiences give people a reason to live; they inspire individual hearts, and often such acts can even capture the heart of a nation. They represent the attainment of the unattainable, and they break new ground for the rest of us. For thousands of years before Edmund Hillary and Tenzing Norgay, no one had ever attained the summit of Mt. Everest. Now, after their achievement in 1953, it is climbed every year.

But there are other ways of actualizing values besides visible achievement. I remember an article called "Doing Good on the Sly" in *Readers Digest* that affected me very much when I was young. The author pointed out that it may never occur to most of us to do something for someone without credit or reward, but that there was an entire world of unspeakable gratitude out there of which we could be a part. If we just gave something unnamed into it, it would return to us in the same way tenfold.

A corollary to this is all those thoughts, words, and deeds that we do not have, the absence of which, almost always unnoticed, makes for a much better world. There is the absence of noise, the absence of ridicule, the absence of ill-judgment, the goal-less enterprise of pure being, where non-attainment, non-grasping, non-doing, and non-achievement shape the course of our experience.

In any case, it was Frankl's point that, while actualizing values was to be preferred over suffering, people almost always have to learn by taking the more difficult path. To actualize what is the highest good within us and to reap meaningful rewards must stand as the great but exceptional achievement against which wash wave after wave of human suffering. Few of us have the luxury or the resources to engineer a pain-free life. Indeed, the great bedfellows of human nature, sloth and torpor, assure that the vast majority of meaningful experiences will come from being extracted out of circumstances that befall us that are beyond our control but that we find some way to surmount. Utopia, in this sense, might be a world in which we have enough forethought to plan ahead, instead of always having to learn painfully from the past.

Suffering, in other words, is inextricably linked to our state of consciousness. While on the one hand, no person is free from suffering, human consciousness seems to have the ability to dissociate itself from painful experiences. Take the case of the American prisoner in a Chinese communist prison during the Korean War. Later interviewed for American public radio, the soldier recounted his horror at hearing a prisoner scream in pain in another part of the building, believing himself to be awakened from sleep by the noise in his cell. A moment later, however, he realized that it was he who was being tortured, he who was screaming. Obviously, as a protective mechanism, depersonalization can periodically set in to rescue us from continuous pain.

Consciousness can also adapt to ever-increasing levels of pain and suffering, as when the body builder or the soldier engages in extreme forms of physical training that seem to most of us to be beyond human endurance, or when rescue attempts under high drama call forth reserves of energy that allow us to dismiss temporarily a broken limb or a gunshot wound or freezing water until the person to be rescued is safe, whereupon we then collapse. As Frankl has shown, even extreme suffering can be a means of transcendence, depending on the attitude we take toward the pain we are called upon to endure.

One reason for this, Swedenborg suggests, is that all events in the natural world conspire to show us what is spiritual.[6] This is because the natural world is derived from the spiritual world, not the other way around. Science, however, tells us that the natural world is really all that exists. Conceptions of God, heaven, or spiritual realms are simply products of the human mind, at best fantasy or imagination. According to this view, we come to believe that the spiritual is derivative of the natural. Swedenborg, however, maintained that exactly the opposite is the case. The spiritual domain expresses itself throughout every aspect of nature in exact correspondence, so that everything in nature corresponds to some aspect in the life of the soul.

An example of the principle of correspondences can be found in homeopathy, the alternative form of medicine that was widely practiced in popular culture in the United States during the early- to mid-nineteenth century and is now experiencing a resurgence in the American counterculture.[7] Originating with the German physician Samuel Hahnemann in the late-eighteenth century, homeopathy treated symptoms by giving minute doses of plant substances that would mimic the presenting symptoms of the patient's illness. The dosage was based on Hahnemann's doctrine of infinitesimals, which dictated that greater dilutions of a substance had a stronger effect on the spiritual body of the patient, the real source of the illness. Treat the spiritual and the physical would also recover.

Contrary to all known medical reason, Hahnemann claimed that the dynamizing function of a drug was achieved when it had been subdivided to its fullest extent. As he stated in *The Organon of Medicine*, the more subtle the drug's action, the higher its curative, spiritual potency, for he believed that it is only by means of the spiritual influence of a morbid agent that our spiritual, vital power can be diseased, and in like manner, only by the spiritual operation of medicine can health be restored.

There can be little doubt that this law of cure was upheld as a belief by doctor and patient alike and, therefore, must have played an important role in harnessing the patient's own resources for self-healing. Hahnemann understood the importance of psychological factors in illness, partly derived, no doubt, during his early career running an asylum for the insane in Germany.

Homeopathy as a medical movement produced a number of important changes in its day. It challenged prevailing allopathic remedies of heroic drugging and started a trend toward the use of diminished quantities of drugs administered in the eradication of disease. It influenced development of the medical procedure for innoculation, which significantly altered the epidemiologic course of numerous malignant diseases. And it anticipated the concept of self-limiting disease—*vis medicatrix natura*—that most illnesses, when left to themselves, will take a prescribed course, often leading to recovery. More importantly, homeopathy became an integral part of the psychological fabric of a variety of folk cultures between 1810 and 1831, when it spread from Germany to France, Russia, Denmark, Spain, Italy, and Great Britain. But it was in the United States that homeopathy gained its widest acceptance.

Hans Birch Gram (1786–1840), a student of Hahnemann, first brought homeopathy to America in the mid-1820s, and is credited with publishing the first treatise on the subject in English, *Ten Characteristics of Homeopathia*, a nearly unreadable translation of one of Hahnemann's essays. Gram first practiced in New York with a small circle of acquaintances who were Swedenborgians. This association was to have important consequences, for homeopathy and Swedenborgianism spread hand-in-hand throughout America, as medical colleges developed in Philadelphia, Cincinnati, Boston, and elsewhere, in many cases involving members of the New Church. The major homeopathic apothecaries in the east—namely, Boericke and Tafel in Philadelphia and Otis Clapp in Boston—were also the major distribution houses in America for Swedenborg's writings.

Eventually, homeopathic treatment was understood against the background of Swedenborg's ideas, such as the doctrine of correspondence.

A reading of contemporary literature in alternative therapies, however, gives no mention of this early association of Swedenborg's psychospiritual philosophy with homeopathic medicine. The principle of correspondence between the natural and the spiritual world is not invoked, nor is the origin of nature in spirit mentioned. Rather, discussions are based on the modern philosophy of medical science that homeopathy works because of purely natural causes; that healing takes place because of some substance the doctor gives the patient; and, consequently, that only what is known within the tradition of allopathic scientific medicine is the real source of healing. I propose a slightly different interpretation, however, one that is preeminently Swedenborgian–namely, while we recognize different kinds of healing, all healing of any kind is essentially spiritual in nature.

Three Types of
Healing

In the various Hindu and Buddhist schools of thought, the conception of disease and death differs vastly from that of the West. In these Eastern philosophies, it is taught that, when we die, we do not pass into eternal life or lay in waiting for the final day of judgment. Rather, after a certain amount of time, either shorter or longer, depending on the school of thought, we are reborn into another form, this time commensurate with the thoughts, words, and deeds of our previous lives. The form will be lower if we have done ill, or higher if we have achieved some measure of enlightenment. Disease and suffering still come to us, but they are the result of what we have done or thought or said, either in this life or a former existence.

This is a profoundly disturbing idea for Westerners to contemplate. Blaming the victim is no explanation for why our loved ones have suffered and died, critics have said. Given what we now know about genetic predispositions, toxic environments, the migration of microbes, and the probability of accidents in a fast-paced technological society, individuals cannot possibly be held responsible for every illness that befalls them.

I maintain, however, that the issue is much more complex, subtle, and mysterious than the superficial explanation that individuals are responsible for their illnesses. I came to this conclusion after working as a consultant with the staff in the Indo-Chinese Refugee Clinic at the Brighton Marine Hospital, a facility available to 18,000 Cambodians in the Boston area, many of whom were victims of the Khmer Rouge genocide.

Many Cambodians seen at the clinic suffered from depression, post-traumatic stress, and other disorders that are the products of systematic torture they endured. When trying to find out the depth of depression, mental-health-care workers cannot simply ask, "Do you ever feel blue?" because Cambodians do not know what this phrase means. Their world view is entirely different. When asked how they felt towards their torturers, for instance, many would say that they held no grudge, or that they wished to exact no revenge. Rather, the victims felt sorry for their tormentors, because the torturers had to bear the consequences of what they had done. When asked why they thought they had been tortured, many Cambodians said that they were given no reason by their torturers, so they believed it must have been for something they had done in a past life that they now had to pay for. These responses startled the mental-health workers, who were unprepared to hear such an explanation after listening to the horrors of what the patient had experienced.

The clue here is that, in the face of the unknown, it may be the attitude we take toward our suffering that allows us to endure. Our state of consciousness might have something to do with our suffering as well as our healing. It seems logical to assume that every illness or trauma is accompanied by an emotional response and that, while we might not have complete control over what happens to us, we do have some measure of control over our emotions.

The Buddhist view expressed by the Cambodians is much more than a mere attitude adjustment, however. Suppose, instead, that the entire universe were structured differently from the way we in the West presume it to be, and that all the reasonable explanations we have in our present state of consciousness are relative and specific to only that state. Despite what we think about ourselves and the superiority of our outlook, from the standpoint of people in other cultures, Western science interprets strictly from its own particular point of view. According to their alternative, non-Western view, science may be relevant in certain domains, but it may not be relevant in all domains of human experience.

In the Buddhist view, for instance, the cause as well as the cure of disease is thought to be profoundly psychological because of the role that consciousness plays in constructing reality. Whatever the large forces of the universe are, they must be co-created in the individual psyche in order to have their malevolent or benevolent effect on an individual. The Swedenborgian minister Warren Felt Evans, who was a pioneer in the American New Thought movement in the late-nineteenth century, took this position when he maintained that health and disease were related to one's internal spiritual state of consciousness. Evans believed that health is the norm, while illness is created by wrong decisions that cut the person off from the natural healing powers of mind and body. Sickness was often the way a person came to meditate on the Divine. At the same time, deliverance from suffering and illness is often initiated by a desire to return to right thoughts and right action; thus, the sick person may promise to set his or her life on a different path if only health would return. In fact, the depths of illness often involve the individual's most basic urges toward life and death. The annals of medicine are full of case histories of people who should have died but lived, because they had hope and the will to live. There are also those who should have lived but died. Because their will or spirit was somehow broken, they gave up the struggle, and expired even when no one expected it. Harnessing the sick person's will to live is certainly central to all healing, although the question of how to instill hope remains a great mystery.

Meanwhile, Western medicine, which has divorced itself from any spiritual references, maintains that disease and illness come to us because of genetic predisposition, accidental contamination, or dangerous conditions. These factors come to us as the result of chance or fate. In general, with the exception of certain lifestyle choices, illness is not equated with consciousness. A person's mental state is generally not thought to have any direct relation to a physical illness, sickness is not regarded as revenge for some act a person has performed, and the patient is generally not thought to be primarily responsible for becoming sick.

Within Christianity, the biblical idea that illness comes to us as punishment for sin goes to the heart of the age-old theological problem of how a benevolent God can wreak such havoc and pain on those very human souls who have committed themselves to his service. In my opinion, Swedenborg gave this idea a profoundly psychological twist when he maintained that, while good and evil do exist, God is the source of all good, but mankind is the source of evil, which comes from the misuse of the capacities of rationality and freedom.

We are free, in other words, to interpret illness in any manner we wish. Typically, in our various states of consciousness, we believe that there are different kinds of suffering. As a result, we can also make these important distinctions between different forms of healing: physical, psychological, and spiritual.

❦ Physical Healing ❧

Physical healing, we believe, involves the alleviation of physical pain. We also think of it as wound healing, as in recovery from an insignificant paper cut or something much more serious, such as a gunshot wound. We could also extend the idea to include recovery from voluntarily inflicted pain for purposes of growth or improvement, such as in the case of orthodontic braces, which have to be periodically tightened to straighten teeth, or brain surgery, in which pain, usually minimized by medications and incidental to the actual cutting of the brain, since there are no pain receptors in brain tissue, is part of the diagnostic and treatment procedure recommended to alleviate some greater kind of suffering, such as death from cancer.

Belief that physical healing requires physical interventions also represents an attitude or way of viewing reality. Our most emblematic example, of course, is Western medicine. According to this philosophy of reality, all disorders of any kind, whether of the body or the mind, are to be treated as biological or chemical in nature. Physical, mental, or spiritual, regardless of complexity, every symptom is always reduced to these terms. The treatment for pain, regardless of its origin, is always aspirin, or stronger analgesics such as the morphine compounds. The treatment for a brain tumor is drugs, surgery, or radiation; for manic-depressive disorders, Lithium; for panic attacks, Inderal. One explanation for alcoholism is that there is a genetic predisposition. Now we are told, there is a gene that predisposes us for depression, schizophrenia, and cancer.

The greatest emphasis in the purely physical approach to healing is placed on the education and experience of the healer. In the case of the Western physician, within the last one hundred years, this has usually involved a college education, attendance at medical school, and a period of hospital residency. The physician is presumed to have mastered logic, mathematics, and the basic sciences associated with chemistry, biology, and physics, even before entering medical school. After introductions to the fundamentals of general medicine, anatomy, physiology, therapeutics, pathology, and diagnosis, the doctor then specializes in some branch of medicine, some being considered more scientific, and therefore more difficult and more prestigious, than others.

The two great paths in the medical profession are scientific research and clinical practice. Basic laboratory research is presumed to produce concrete and repeatable evidence that can be applied to patient care in clinical settings. Where there is such evidence, there is a general agreement within the scientific and medical community for a specific type of treatment. This agreement justifies the use of tested methods on patients by only qualified physicians in approved clinical settings, such as a hospital or an office.

Thus, the Western physician is trained in a particular cultural tradition that values rational thinking and sensory measurement over intuitional or emotive kinds of approaches. These latter approaches are, of course, present, but generally de-emphasized, perhaps emerging as a byproduct of good scientific care. The rational-empirical approach, then, is organized around an accepted body of proven scientific evidence that is delivered under strict supervision regarding the quality of care and the requisite level of medical expertise.

Under these circumstances, what the physician does is considered to be the causative agent that heals the patient. Health and illness are understood in terms of the manipulation of organs, tissues, cells, and molecules by chemical, mechanical, electrical, or surgical means. The physician's interventions are active, while the patients are asked to adopt a passive attitude by submitting to the diagnostic procedures and following the treatment regime. In this way, the physician is always able to give a scientific explanation for the cause of the illness, and there is always a scientific intervention that is supposed to effect a cure. Surgical anesthesia, the antiseptic hospital environment, the germ theory of disease, the "magic-bullet" theory are all products of scientific thinking and define the parameters of physical healing.

ℒ Psychological Healing ℛ

Psychological healing, we have come to believe, involves the treatment of pain that comes from anguish and conflict. It is the treatment of ideas with ideas. One example is the use of psychotherapy to uncover the causes of emotional turmoil that can change the chemical composition of the body over long periods, perhaps enough to cause ulcers, high blood pressure, or more serious conditions. Fear is a psychological condition that can cause great suffering, as can great hatred, especially when this feeling persists for long periods. Psychological trauma often accompanies great physical injuries; but the aftereffects, which might involve depression, grief, loss of self-esteem, or recurring fears, often go untreated.

The most important source of psychological suffering is intrapsychic conflict. This occurs when there is a prolonged contradiction between two ideas we hold in the same field of consciousness, or it could be a clash between two different systems of thought. It could also be a conflict between the intellect and the emotions, or between the mind and the body within the same field of personality. Intrapsychic conflict can also come about when a life crisis arises, such as the impending death of a loved one, where a caregiver may be called on to carry out normal functions under abnormal conditions. Emotional and intellectual anguish may result; if persistent over time, anguish may be manifested as physical symptoms.

Within the fields of psychology and psychiatry, the conversion of psychological ideas to physical symptoms is called the psychogenic hypothesis. Psychogenesis, meaning "psychological in origin," refers to the perceptions we have of stress, trauma, and pain, particularly how our perceptions become transformed after prolonged periods into the physical symptoms of common illness or into the repetitive habits of the neurotic.

One hundred years ago, the psychogenic hypothesis was explained in terms of fragments of our personality that had split off from the waking state. Experiences that we could not normally integrate into our worldview would split away from the larger picture that we construct of reality and float around in the subconscious, acting according to laws of their own. A sexual trauma, for instance, might be repressed in some subconscious region and, in this condition, rob waking consciousness of part of its energy. Meanwhile, this lost memory might continually draw similar experiences of a lesser intensity to it, until, eventually, a large mass of experiences were collected around a core. This aggregation was called an unconscious complex.

Complexes were thought to reveal themselves to waking consciousness in a number of ways. They might appear in the form of a minor symptom, such as the appearance of a facial rash on the eve of an important date or laryngitis at the moment of an important speech; or they might appear in a major episode, such as in cases of multiple personality, when a complex bursts forth and captures the entire field of awareness, presenting itself as a completely coherent and independent identity.

Ideas were thought to produce psychological symptoms of neurosis, meaning symptoms that were thought to have no known biological origin. Over the past one hundred years, the psychogenic hypothesis has gradually come to be applied as well to physical illness. In the 1930s, the major psychosomatic illnesses were considered ulcerative colitis, hypertension, and low back pain. Now, focus has shifted to the psychological components of major physical illness, such as heart attack and cancer.

A recent and quite graphic example was presented at a case conference on Behavioral Medicine at Boston University Hospital. A nurse in her twenties suffered from herpes simplex, a virus difficult to eliminate, the symptoms of which flare up under stressful circumstances. Each month the woman traveled a hundred miles to visit her mother, with whom she had numerous unresolved interpersonal problems. Her facial skin was clear and smooth when she left; but, in the hour-and-a-half it took to get to her mother's house, her skin became progressively filled with herpes sores. She endured this unsightly and embarrassing condition for the entire weekend. When she had to return to the city where she lived, she would get in the car, her face all broken out, and begin driving. As she drove, the facial blemishes would disappear, until she arrived at her home, with a clean and smooth face. This problem continued as long as she was required to make her monthly trips.

❦ Spiritual Healing ❧

Thus, we believe that physical healing requires physical medicine, while psychological healing involves using the powers of consciousness to address problems that have arisen from psychological causes. Spiritual healing, however, appears to be quite different in both attitude and experience from its counterparts in the physical and psychological domains. Indeed, the assumptions regarding the very nature of reality are so radically different that those who believe in spiritual healing might at first appear totally unrelated to other types of healers. This is because both physical and psychological healing are predicated on the assumption that suffering is the result of natural causes or traumatic experiences and that, once these causes are known, adequate interventions can be developed for their alleviation.

The philosophical struggle between medical physicians and psychologists is a matter of whether one gives credibility to the view that ideas and emotions can have physical consequences. The physicalist may presume that a vague term like "the mind" actually refers to nothing but the reaction of chemicals with each other. If consciousness does have some palpable existence, it is always dependent on the biological functioning of the physical organism. At best, according to this view, consciousness is a mere byproduct of our physiology, not a cause of it. The psychologist, on the other hand, claims causal efficacy for the powers of consciousness. That means consciousness, in the form of decisions, impulses, feelings, and actions, can have effects in the physical domain. In both cases, however, suffering is alleviated because of mastery over the material or psychological environment. Pain is presumed to have an understandable cause, or at least an understandable intervention.

With spiritual healing, however, the source of all understanding is unknowable, ineffable, inconceivable. We cannot control that which is greater than ourselves, especially that which is presumed to be our very source. Physical and psychological healing are predicated on the assumptions that the natural world is primary and that human beings are objects in nature to be studied, while conceptions of the spirit are believed to be merely ideas we have formulated from the exercise of our imagination. Spiritual healing, however, is predicated on exactly the opposite: the phenomena of the natural world not only have no independent existence apart from the domain of the spirit, but the physical world before us is really pure spirit, disguised in natural form.

In spiritual healing, the domain of the spirit is primary, the only reality; the domain of the natural is illusory, or at best inconsequential. Healing, whether physical or mental, takes place when we come into the full presence of the Divine, when we cast away our illusion and enter into the wider domain of the highest and the best that is possible to experience. The nature of this spiritual domain is undefiled, ecstatic, pure, all-loving, and illuminating. When we come into the presence of what is divinely highest, we are healed. When we are exposed to its light, which is in everything and everyone, all physical and mental infirmity falls away. This is because we see who we truly are and we see the essential and true nature of all reality—love, bliss, light, heaven.

We may try to get to this state on our own. Usually, however, we need a guide or ally of some sort to show the way, to calm our fears until the obstacles fall from our interior vision. Healing in this sense means allowing; it is showing a sick person the path and correcting wrong impressions about the ultimate nature of all things. From this standpoint, we can then see that the healing of the scientific physician is quite accidental. The physician says, "This is what I did that healed the patient." What the physician actually did was to lead the ill person into the domain of hope, of compassion, of freedom from all suffering; for the experience of our humanity is always the path toward this higher light. A mystery healed the person, not the doctor's manipulations. It was the union of personalities that allowed the sick person to transcend the confines of the natural world and to gain access to these higher spiritual domains.

❦ All Healing Is Spiritual ❧

If we consider this point of view for a moment, we see that, from the phenomenological standpoint of a psychology of inner experience, all forms of healing are essentially spiritual in nature. Every single kind of healing, whether we are talking about band-aids and iodine, psychotherapy, or the water cure at Lourdes, is just as much a part of the greater miracle of reality as any other form of healing. An opening of the internal doors of perception is required, however, to see that the domain of the spirit infuses all aspects of material life. As I interpret

Swedenborg's psychology, particularly that found in the interchapter material of the *Arcana Coelestia*, a radical separation between the natural and the spiritual exists only in the unenlightened condition.[1] Under the circumstances of normal waking consciousness, it appears that no other superior state than the rational exists, so no other explanation for anything except a natural one seems possible. But once there is an opening of the internal doors of perception, every natural occurrence is seen as a manifestation of some aspect of the internal spiritual domain. Nature is no longer looked at as separate from divinity. Rather, we are then able to see that divinity lies all around us, only the rest of society remains too hidebound to accept that fact. We then live at every moment in that wider spiritual domain, only appearing to our compatriots to move in the natural world alone. Meanwhile, according to our own perceptions, we put in the usual good day's work in the mundane world, knowing all the time that we are surrounded by nothing less than the angels and that we ourselves and others around us are, in reality, sparks of the Divine.

4

The Role of
Belief

To understand the role of belief in healing, we
must acknowledge the reality of the unconscious.
Below the surface of consciousness, we have constructed an elaborate network of ideas and concepts that
form the framework of our attitudes. Over a lifetime,
this network tends to become a massive, overburdened,
encrusted hulk, which works the same way every time.
Continuity results on one hand, but colossal rigidity results on the other. Thus, the role of belief in healing can
work both ways—a well-developed worldview is sometimes the best medicine against illness, while at the same
time overly rigid habits, especially those involving
lifestyle choice, can become the chronic cause of illnesses that are a long time in the making. In these terms,
our beliefs can become a life-and-death matter.

Normally our attention is centered on what our sense organs are attached to in the external material world and the thoughts and perceptions we have of these sensations, which occupy center stage in our awareness. Characteristically, the reader focuses on the words on the page, scanning from left to right in a continuous flow. Simultaneously, as the words are being translated by waking consciousness, grammatical sentences become thoughts. So at any given moment, there are two streams intermingling: the stream of words and sentences and the stream of thoughts that we weave in between to translate the words into meaningful ideas.

We might also say that, as the words and the ideas flow by, they intermingle into a larger stream of understanding. Each idea appeals to us in some way, some more than others. We can catch a glimpse of this appeal as the words flow by when we shift our attention from the words and ideas themselves to the feelings we have for each idea as we grasp it. Some ideas are boring, some interesting; some arouse feelings of disgust, others delight. Whatever they do, the emotions color each thought in the process of creating meaning, giving that thought warmth in a way that leads us to identify the thoughts we are having as our own. The thoughts are not just cold ideas existing in a vacuum, but they are rich with blood, so to speak, engorged in a halo of emotions that flow onward with the thoughts. So it is appropriate, as William James once said, to speak not only of the stream of thought, but also of the stream of feeling.

The experience of the feelings that attach themselves to each passing thought takes us to the periphery of immediate waking consciousness. In feelings, we approach closer to the barrier or filtering mechanism that separates consciousness from the unconscious. On this side of the barrier, we recognize the incoming stimuli from the outer world, the rational ordering of thoughts, the recall of familiar memories, and the first and last steps in innumerable chains of habits that make up our familiar responses to day-to-day events, among others. On the other side of the barrier, we have a vast network of mental structures built up over a lifetime: a congestion of categories, discriminations, and fixed ideas in which we have pigeonholed every experience, all of which are arranged in what appears to be permanently fixed positions in relation to one another.

For example, each time we look at a chair, we first see the chair in front of us, and then we experience all the chairs we have ever seen, a concept that is the vast cubbyhole in our mind into which we have slipped just this perception, so that we can identify this object in front of us as a chair. When we do that, we no longer see a chair in front of us, but rather we experience the category of chair in our mind, containing the memory of all the chairs we have ever experienced. We believe the object before our eyes to be a chair because it conforms in our mind to all the other chairs we have ever seen.

In this belief, we find satisfaction, calmness, security, even happiness because confirmation that every time we see a chair it is still a chair means that the world is in order—regular, predictable, unchanging. A chair is always a chair. I remember one time, however, sitting down on something that I thought was a chair when it really was not. My reaction was, of course, surprise, which I experienced as I pitched over onto the floor. There were several reasons for my reaction: I did not expect to fall; I was worried that I might hurt myself until I discovered how I was going to land; I was also embarrassed at my gracelessness, all in addition to the experience of my misperception. The thought that the chair was not the chair seemed inconsequential at first, but the effects of that fact certainly were instantaneous and complex in terms of the unexpected worlds they immediately called forth. I had, after all, fallen into the unknown, as the familiar world around me suddenly disappeared. My belief in the reality of the chair was being tested, and the belief failed the test.

We now have a number of interesting points before us in order to understand the role of belief in healing. The first might be that, out of the blooming, buzzing confusion, we attend to what we are interested in. Out of the great mass of incoming stimuli, our prior beliefs and attitudes heavily condition what we will see and pay attention to. Changing our reactions to things might lie in getting back to the basic attitudes and beliefs that make us react in one way rather than another.

Another important point is that beliefs arise from at least two sources: external norms set by our cultural surroundings, which we internalize into our own personal structures of awareness, and internal norms established as the result of the depth of our interior experience. According to the rules and regulations of survival in our family, village, tribe, and nation, healing in contemporary American culture most often means band-aids and prescriptions, thermometers and scalpels; doctors who have traditionally been men and nurses who have traditionally been women; hospitals outfitted with the latest scientific and medical technology; or clinics where a band of psychotherapists and family counselors sit to listen to our problems for fifty minutes. Many of us grew up going to the same doctor our parents went to, someone who was known to our family, who practiced a kind of medicine that everyone else around us believed in. We may or may not have believed in the healing powers of the school nurse, but she was always there as a symbol, reminding us that there was a sentinel on guard in case we were injured. Despite the fact that health care today has become chaotic and, when forced into a health maintenance organization, we may not get our first choice of doctors, Western medicine is the norm.

Thus, we absorb whatever the external, socio-cultural standards are over the course of a lifetime. However, we always temper them with the depth of our own personal experience, with the amount of self-understanding that we bring to each thought, word, or deed. In my opinion, the deeper the level of self-knowledge and the more unfathomable one's experience has been in looking within, the more interior, rather than exterior, experiences are used as the standard by which to believe and to act in any given situation.

Here, I believe, is the most fundamental problem in all debates about ethics. The question of how to act in a given situation is generally discussed in terms of the internalization of external norms. We simply have no context to understand how actions and beliefs can be guided by the depth of noetic or internal visionary experiences. But it is probably correct to say that beliefs—in general, being internal and subjective—are ruled more by sentiment, feeling, and previous experience, especially if they were of a vivid nature, than by a set of external rules that we have internalized.

The course chosen in the treatment of ill-health is a prime example. The path is usually going to be one the person believes in. A case study is myself. I sustained a traumatic neck injury as a senior in high school when I fell off a trampoline in gym class. From the diagnosis that followed, I learned that the sixth and seventh cervical vertebrae had been crushed together, destroying the lubricating disc in between. The prescribed treatment was confinement in a Robinson brace, which immobilized my neck for almost four months. For the recurrent pain, I was given regular doses of Norgesic, a combination muscle relaxer, painkiller, and heavy-duty aspirin compound. Subsequent yearly x-rays showed progressive post-traumatic arthritis. Eventually, because I was not guided into any kind of systematic physical rehabilitation, the muscles in my back began to lock up, and I started to loose the ability to lift objects with my right arm. After three years of increasing discomfort and frustration because I had to stay on medication while the physicians treating me could only manage a worsening situation, I resolved to forego further x-rays and drug treatments. At the same time, I began taking regular yoga classes three and four times a week.

This decision had been building for some time, as I had been studying the *raja* yoga texts in my comparative religion courses, had become interested in the conceptualizations that yoga presented regarding the nature of insight and pure consciousness, and had been thinking about learning the *asanas*, or postures. This decision was not exactly an irrecoverable break with Western medicine, however, but only an abandonment of a long program of misdirected treatment that had proved a failure for that specific disorder. The only difference was that, instead of switching physicians or changing the kind and level of medication, I switched healing traditions and went into a nontraditional, non-Western mode of thinking.

In this altogether new frame of reference, I attached myself to an expert teacher, began a regulated discipline of physical exercises, coupled these exercises with intensive meditation, and widened my reading of the history and philosophy behind these practices. In short, I switched my attention to an altogether different belief system. I spent two-and-a-half years in this alternative mode of rehabilitation and, after my recovery through yoga, went on to training in the martial arts. I have had no trouble with my neck in any way since then, which was almost twenty-five years ago.

This suggests yet another part that belief plays in the healing process, namely, that one way to test the truth of a belief is to look at its consequences. What we say, what we think, and what we do, all may change periodically or appear now to be this and now to be that, apparently contradicting what we did yesterday. But part of the underlying stability of who we are is the embeddedness of our attitudes and our belief systems. If we believe in alternative forms of healing, it is usually because, in the past, we have had positive successful experiences thinking in this way that have been strongly reinforced by recovery of health. Here is a man who has recovered from inoperable stomach cancer using meditation, herbs, and prayer. Next to him is a woman whose cancer has gone into remission because she put her faith solely in Western science, believing that alternative therapies were completely useless. Both have had successful experiences that, for the time being, have reinforced not only their respective lifestyles but also their radically different worldviews.

Another element of belief worth noting relates to the spiritual qualities of faith and hope. We are perpetually told that science deals only with the hard facts, while religion deals with faith. This is, of course, not exactly true, since the scientist has faith in his own methods, believes in the picture of the physical world created by his science, invests a significant amount of objective certainty in the consistently measurable outcome of his studies, hopes that his experiments will turn out as expected, and so on. These are all clearly the qualities of faith from a psychological point of view. Faith communities bound by common religious beliefs, on the other hand, are constantly looking for empirical ways to corroborate their hopes and dreams—proof of life after death, some visible sign that God has been here, evidence that a particular belief is true, and so on. The center of gravity may be different, but the two enterprises of science and religion represent individuals who constantly demonstrate faith in what they do.

Faith and hope, psychologically speaking, are states of mind invested with an extraordinary amount of positive feeling. When your mother called your name when you were little, you had faith that it was always going to be the same face when you turned to her expectantly and asked, "What?" There was also always expectancy there, since you did not know what she wanted until she followed with a complete sentence. Faith is believing something will come about not because of hard, cold facts, which themselves may be only probability statements; it is believing that something will come about because of an intuitive sense we extend to some event that becomes part of the conditions necessary for that event to be created. Things that are at any minute in a potential state of coming into being are actually helped to come into being when we invest our attention in them. Consciousness, especially with regard to internal events, co-creates phenomena; without it, certain kinds of realities, especially those of inner states of consciousness, will simply not come about.

The attitude of passive volition in the field of biofeedback studies is an example.[1] Also called the voluntary control of internal states, biofeedback uses electronic monitoring equipment to show a person his or her own heart rate, blood pressure, breathing patterns, and so on. It has been established that giving this kind of information feedback to patients allows them to use the readings to raise or lower different physiological processes over which they would not normally have conscious control.

For example, a woman, wired to monitoring devices and usually reclining, is first taken through a series of relaxation techniques and then shown continuous readings of, say, her beating heart. She can make her heart speed up by thinking of some exciting event, or slow down by taking deep, relaxed breaths for several minutes. She can also make the dial go in a desired direction using the intentional capacities of consciousness—that is, by willing the dial one way or the other. To do this, however, she must desire the end, and then relax and forget it. This is much like making a wish. She conceives a desire and then consecrates the wish to fate. A period of forgetfulness often intervenes, but the original wish is then remembered if the desired outcome happens to come about.

In the case of biofeedback, the patient sets his or her desire in mind and then relaxes and forgets it. A short time later, the desired result comes about. This is called passive volition, the opposite of active volition, which occurs when we command that something be done and it comes about. Passive volition occurs when we ask for something to come about, and, a little while later, it happens. High-powered business executives, for instance, typically overexert themselves on the biofeedback machines trying to get their heart rates to go down. They are used to applying direct influence over events to make situations come out in their own predefined way. However, the more the executives exert themselves the more the heart rate goes up, because human beings normally do not have direct voluntary control over such involuntary systems as circulation. Their efforts at control, in this case, produce stress instead of relaxation because they are thwarted from their goal. Finally, they get so frustrated that they give up in disgust. At that point, their heart rate begins to fall. The feedback they get from the monitor indicates that they are achieving their goal by letting go, not by seizing control. To continue to guide this force toward the desired end means that they have to learn how to ask their bodies to relax and then give the time to let it happen. Eventually, if they can keep letting go, they may be astonished at their ability to reduce their heart rates. But they will have to harness a completely unused part of their personality to do it—the permitting, forgiving, asking, hopeful, and faith-filled side.

Here, the perceptive reader will see analogies to the attitude of prayer. We must believe as an act of faith, not as an act of certainty; we must put ourselves in the right attitude of humility and respect, which is not a narcissistic posturing; we must learn to ask instead of command. Then, of course, we must wait. This waiting must be carried on with patience, not impatience. And we should be prepared in the event that our prayer, whatever it is, might not be answered. These characteristics are similar to the kind of passive volition in biofeedback studies that leads eventually to the voluntary control of internal states.

But perhaps the most important implication stemming from the attitude of faith and hope is the essential boundlessness of subjective experiential consciousness. Theologically, at least from a Christian perspective, this is expressed as the omnipresence of the Creator in every place, all at once, and for all time, in which the reach of God has no end. A boundless faith is required to meet the Divine. Psychologically, we are confronted with the essentially unfathomable nature of the unconscious, the sense of timelessness that comes from journeying into the interior reaches of the mind.

From a scientific standpoint, however, interior boundlessness is purely absurd. While the physical universe is conceived as essentially limitless, there is no comparable interior domain, no parallel universe in consciousness, no interior states of awareness other than the one we use to understand the dimensions of the physical world. For those who have experienced what Aldous Huxley called an opening of the internal doors of perception, however, the interior dimension of consciousness is every bit as real as the merely physical world; meanwhile, the physical scientists are denied access to it by their commitment to a contrary set of assumptions about the nature of reality.

Occasionally, some scientists break away and venture into uncharted territory. But the way that the basic science community deals with such errant believers is to excommunicate them, so their subject matter never has to be considered. John Cunningham Lilly, a neurophysiologist who perfected the floating tank experiments in sensory isolation before turning to interspecies communication with dolphins, is one of my favorite examples of such an adventurous scientist. In his work *The Center of the Cyclone*, Lilly recounts how he embarked on a course different from other sensory-deprivation studies.[2] When other researchers studied sensory deprivation by locking their subjects up in dark rooms, immobilizing them with restraints, and pumping propaganda in their ears, the subjects reported negative experiences. Lilly, however, built flotation tanks with breathing apparatus so the subjects could hang suspended in the water for hours. The experience was so blissful that even other scientists wanted to be subjects in his experiments. His major conclusion was that, given the optimal conditions for exploration, within the province of the mind, what one believes to be true either is true or becomes true within the limits of one's own experiential and experimental possibilities—simply because one feels under such circumstances that, within the province of the mind, there are no limits.

❧ Benson's Remembered Wellness ❧

No more important example advocating the biological power of belief has recently appeared than the work of Dr. Herbert Benson, a cardiologist at Harvard Medical School and director of the Mind-Body Medical Institute at Deaconness/Beth Israel Hospital. Benson began scientific studies on transcendental meditators—followers of the teachings of Maharishi Mahesh Yogi—in the late 1960s, and measured several important physiological changes that occurred as a result of practicing meditation. Among other things, his subjects, even beginners in the practice, exhibited lowered heart rate, lowered blood pressure, and lowered metabolism, as measured by a decrease in oxygen and carbon dioxide consumption. Benson called this effect of meditation the Relaxation Response.

Subsequent investigation also found that these changes could persist over the long term and that systematic practice of the Relaxation Response could have beneficial effects on health. Hypertensive subjects on medication who learned the response and practiced it for two twenty-minute periods each day were eventually able to cut their medication dosage in half. Patients suffering from migraine, heart disease, and other coronary ailments were likewise helped. Practicing the Relaxation Response was found to be beneficial in controlling the severity of symptoms in premenstrual syndrome and other disorders where pain control was needed.

Eventually, Benson came to believe that the Relaxation Response was a natural body reflex exactly opposite from what has been called the fight-flight reflex. The fight-flight reflex is the body's natural protective response to stress. This reflex throws the system into high gear in preparation for attack and defense against impending danger or high-speed flight from it. Chemicals are dumped into the blood for ready use in creating energy; the person goes on high alert, as it were. High-stress situations that perpetuate a constant state of such alertness, however, eventually lead to breakdown of the body and possibly even death. Evidently, the Relaxation Response checks this process and resets the neurological thermostat so that the body remains at a calmer level of daily functioning, despite the pressures around it.

Because a person's lifestyle reflects his or her worldview, episodes of illness involving issues of life and death invoke a person's ultimate beliefs. For this reason, Benson advised his patients to associate practice of the Relaxation Response with prayers, chants, or phrases drawn from their own religious tradition. In this way, beliefs and healing become positively associated.

Benson detailed his findings in his works *The Relaxation Response* and *Your Maximum Mind*. In a more recent work, *Timeless Healing*,[3] Benson has taken the discussion a step farther by investigating what scientists call the placebo effect, or the element of suggestibility exhibited by a patient. For example, a man goes to a physician with a headache. The doctor gives him a white pill to take; he takes it, and his headache goes away. The patient is unaware, however, that the pill is merely sugar, not aspirin. Be that as it may, the man came expecting to get a pill that would make him well; he remembered that aspirin was a white pill. Because he believed the pill was aspirin, his headache went away. To one group of physicians, this is charlatanry; to another, it represents harnessing the patients' own capacity to heal themselves.

The placebo effect has become an important influence that must be controlled for, especially in scientific studies that administer drugs for particular disorders. Some patients will always get better just because they are receiving medication, regardless of what it is. To account for the placebo effect, scientists often give the real drug to half the number of patients in a scientific study, while the other half are given a placebo, but no one knows who got what until the outcome is tabulated. The results of this are thought to be more accurate because the placebo response has been measured in the one group along with the real effect of the drug in the other.

Benson's contention, however, is that we should first learn to harness the patient's expectations for health and use them more systematically in the healing process. More importantly, he believes that what we now somewhat derisively call the placebo effect is actually a very old genetic memory of wellness. The patient's expectation is not merely a thin hope that he or she will get well; it is an archetypal remembrance, built into the genes, of what health feels like. Thus, what the patient invokes in a personal expectation of recovery is an experience universal to all human beings. This is partly the meaning of the medical adage *vis medicatrix natura*, that left to themselves, most disorders will run their course and the organism will get well naturally, a concept we referred to previously in discussing homeopathy. According to Benson, we must open ourselves to this genetic memory and learn to remember what it is like to be well. We must believe we can become well if it is going to happen.

As any good psychotherapist knows, however, the act of changing beliefs involves getting into the unconscious and into the maze of interrelated structures that make up our attitudes and value systems. Modern psychologists know only a small bit about changing beliefs, mainly by what they have learned from studying conditioned habits in rats, called behaviorism, which they have now applied to humans, called cognitive psychology, and from their investigations of returning prisoners of war subjected to propaganda and brainwashing. But to change attitudes truly, to redeploy the internal structures completely and begin again, consciousness must turn in upon itself. As long as attention stays fixed on external reality, the structures of the mind remain fixed. But let attention turn within, and old habits, intricately built networks of attitudes, and the entire infrastructure of analytic discriminations begin to shift. When that happens a little, we have insight; when that happens a lot, we have spiritual transformation. In any event, the road inward leads toward an opening of the internal sense. When we experience this opening, the first thing we encounter is the domain of the imaginal.

The Domain of the Imaginal

I n the Indian system of yoga, the act of turning inward is called *pratyahara*. It means that, instead of attending to what goes on in the external world of the
senses and the intellect, attention turns inward to its own
physiological and psychological processes. This may
seem at first impossible to do, but the yogis actually
mean something quite practical by this idea.[1] In the first
place, we normally remain unconscious of the way our
senses remain attached to objects in the external world.
In yoga, attention is drawn to the feelings of pleasure or
pain we experience when we call forth each object. Normally, when we smell bread baking, we walk to the
kitchen to find out where it is, inquire of the cook when
it will be ready, anticipate a taste of that first bite, and
maybe even envision ourselves consuming the whole
loaf. Attention in this case remains with the object,

helped along by the intense pleasure of smelling the bread and reinforced even more by the anticipation of eating it, which seem only to lead to even more imaginal productions.

The yogi, however, would ask us to begin our meditation by attending not to the source of the smell—the bread—but to look back into ourselves, into the act of smelling. Likewise, when we hear someone call our name, attention would be drawn not to the caller, but to the apparatus within us that is doing the hearing. When we taste our breakfast in the morning, the focus would be not on the food, but on the taste buds and the nasal sinuses and the feel of the food as it goes through our bodies. When we begin to attend to what goes on within, we are inevitably led back to the mind as an object of study. And as I have said in the previous chapter, it is a basic principle of psychotherapy, medical psychology, and spiritual practice that, when consciousness becomes conscious of itself, it becomes something else. In this movement is the beginning of all transformation and all healing.

By the opening of the internal spiritual sense, I believe that Swedenborg meant that a true change in consciousness takes place when we shift our attention from an exclusive focus on the external material world and embark upon the inward journey of spiritual development. Under most circumstances, however, especially in the beginning, special techniques are needed in order to gain access into these internal domains. In Swedenborg's case, it was his use of a primitive but highly effective form of dream interpretation.

When this opening of the internal spiritual sense happened to him personally, Swedenborg was already a mature man and a distinguished scientist used to disciplined inquiry. He had embarked on a quest when he was a young man to grasp all the known sciences of his day. As a student at the University of Uppsala in the early 1700s, he began with the study of mathematics, astronomy, geology, and mineralogy, and then began writing about the philosophical implications of this new knowledge for understanding the soul. This, of course, would be out of the question in the science of today, but most scientists in Swedenborg's time regarded science has having profound spiritual implications and wrote about them. The botanist Carolus Linnaeus, for instance, who was Swedenborg's contemporary and related to him by marriage, viewed the plant kingdom within a much more vast hierarchy of God's plan for man than do present-day botanists who still use his system of classification.

But Swedenborg felt that his scientific knowledge was still incomplete. Thus, embarking on an extensive study of anatomy and physiology, he turned from the inorganic to the organic world, studying throughout Europe in the early 1700s. He mastered among other talents the art of lens grinding, and he also attached himself to the microscopist Hermann Boerhaave, constructing his own microscope. With this instrument, he amassed all that was known in his day about the body in a physiological encyclopedia. By so doing, he was also able to make several minor contributions to the history of medicine, particularly in his identification of the thebecian veins and his conclusions on cerebral circulation.

Beyond anatomy and physiology, we have said, Swedenborg pressed on to a study of sensory psychology, which focused on the senses and the rational intellect. Here, however, his scientific investigations took a completely new turn, because he had finally come to the mind itself as an object of analytic study, the very source of his subject matter and his method. The problem was whether to continue objectifying the mind into more and more logical categories of analysis, or to confront consciousness wholly and directly. He pursued the latter of the two choices, realizing that he had essentially reached the limit of a purely impersonal approach. The subject of his inquiry was nothing less than the depths of his own experience. He would have to learn how faithfully to allow his experiences to occur, understanding that analysis was not the only possible state of consciousness.

To navigate how consciousness was going to catch a glimpse of itself, Swedenborg employed a primitive but workable form of dream interpretation, as he detailed in his *Journal of Dreams*.[2] Dreams are, after all, halfway between waking and sleep, capturing the energic power of the unconscious and expressing in disguised, symbolic forms what is normally uncognizable to consciousness. And most importantly, they gave Swedenborg a way to gain a modicum of control over the dialogue between consciousness and the unconscious.

His method was quite simple. First, he paid attention to his dreams. That is, dreaming became a conscious intention. Put another way, in the waking state, he generated the wish to have his attention now focus on his own dreaming behavior. This is important, because normally waking consciousness remains captivated by external stimuli and generally ignores its own dreams.

Second, he wrote down whatever he dreamt. This meant that, while he experienced the dream in one state of consciousness, as soon as he had awakened, he transferred as much of the content as he could remember to writing. This commitment actually had two consequences. One was that, once he intended to remember his dreams, he not only began to remember them but he also began to remember more of them. Another was that this commitment led him to realize the absolute honesty he had to marshal in order to record just what he remembered, with as little elaboration or censorship as possible.

He soon realized that analyzing the content of the dream was a separate operation from both dreaming or recording. Dreaming essentially represents an intuitive condition, while recording is clear observation. Meanwhile, analysis calls for entirely different faculties, especially those of logic, generalization, and judgment. As if he were an external observer whose objectivity had to be kept at all costs in his analysis, Swedenborg accepted unflinchingly what the record told him about himself.

In this way, a doorway opened between consciousness and the unconscious. Swedenborg began to see the unconscious through the reflective mechanism of his own dreams; and soon, as a result, he experienced an opening of the internal sense. It was as if, whenever he looked out onto the external and the visible, the three-dimensional world suddenly took on a fourth dimension. Objects that before had only length, width, and depth, now also took on an interior aspect. This is the dimension of consciousness where awareness contributes to the perception of the object. He understood that there never can be a world of identifiable objects without some consciousness somewhere to perceive them. At the same time, the interior domain became visible to him. When consciousness turned its attention within, worlds within worlds suddenly were laid out—internal dimensions of experience opened, all of which he resolved to explore.

❧ The Hypnagogic State ❧

Whatever the intrinsic connection between consciousness and healing, the hypnagogic state, the twilight region between waking and sleeping that we pass through twice a day, seems to be the primary doorway through which consciousness must pass in order to enter into alternative realities. Similarly, the hypnagogic state has long been understood as a domain of therapeutic healing, as I have discussed in my work *William James on Exceptional Mental States.*[3]

The question of how often and in what way we enter the hypnagogic state is an important one. Traditional studies on sleep research indicate that infants pass through this zone quite frequently; adults enter it only twice daily, once in the morning and once at night; and the elderly, especially the very old, appear to revert back to the original patterns of childhood and infancy.

As every parent knows, newborn babies sleep in what researchers have called a polyphasic sleeping cycle. They are up for two hours, sleep for two hours, up for two hours, and then sleep for two hours again, eight to twelve times in a twenty-four hour cycle. Because of socialization and chemical adjustments that the baby is making to the light/dark cycle, within a few weeks or months, the baby begins waking up fewer and fewer times at night, until the child is sleeping all night long and awake during the day, precisely the schedule of the parents. This is a diphasic sleeping cycle. This cycle continues until the last phase of old age, when, depending on many factors that will either prolong or shorten the periods of alert wakefulness, the person reverts back to the polyphasic sleeping cycle.

Throughout these changes, the person spontaneously enters the hypnagogic state each time he or she enters or leaves deep sleep. We know this from classic studies measuring brain-wave activity during both sleep and wakefulness with an electroencephalogram (EEG). Characteristically, during the waking state, when analytic activity is at its highest, the EEG shows that the cerebral cortex of the normal person generates a high frequency of electrical impulses called beta waves. Beta waves are characteristic when the person engages in mathematical calculations, for instance.

During relaxed alertness, however, when nothing in particular fills the center of attention, but the person remains aware of everything that is going on in the immediate surroundings, a slightly lower frequency of impulses is generated called alpha waves. While these are the waves most often associated with quiet, restful meditation, most people can begin to generate alpha waves immediately just by shutting their eyes. A disturbance of any kind while the eyes remain shut, such as a loud noise, will immediately cause the alpha waves to cease, a process called alpha blocking. Within a few minutes, however, after the disturbance ceases, the alpha waves resume.

A person is usually found to be in a light state of sleep when the brain waves get slower and deeper, beyond alpha. At this level, theta waves predominate. These are most closely associated with dreaming, daytime reveries, and other forms of mental imagery. Characteristically during dreaming, the person's eyes flutter, a condition called rapid eye movements, or REM sleep. These eye movements also occur in conjunction with visual scenes the person witnesses during dreaming.

Beyond theta-wave states of dreaming, the person falls into deep sleep, the deepest sleep of the night. Sometimes REM activity goes on here, but the characteristic EEG patterns, called delta waves, are very slow and of the lowest frequency. Researchers do not believe that normal thinking or imaging goes on in this state. As sleep both conserves and restores energy, deep sleep is thought to give the profoundest state of rest, a state completely absent of consciousness and memory. Transcendental meditation researchers, however, believe that they can generate delta waves in deep states of meditation, a supposed fourth state of consciousness that is not identical to waking, sleep with dreams, or deep, profound sleep without dreams.

But, as far as the hypnagogic state is concerned, sleep studies indicate that, in the course of a normal diurnal cycle—that is, one in which the person is awake for sixteen hours during the day and asleep for eight hours at night—waking consciousness dominated by beta activity is followed by alpha-theta activity characteristic of the hypnagogic state. On first falling asleep, we pass through this condition very quickly, however, and, in the first twenty-to-sixty minutes of a good night's sleep, fall immediately into deep delta.

After this first long initial period, we return again to the surface of consciousness, hovering just below the margin, not yet awake, but in a light state of sleep. In this condition, we begin to again generate alpha and theta waves. It is here that REM sleep also begins, which has led researchers to conclude that dreaming is primarily a characteristic of the hypnagogic state. Characteristically, REM activity at this level continues for only a few moments, before the individual plunges again into deep delta, this time for a period from ten-to-thirty minutes. After this, the person again rises to alpha-theta and REM activity. This continues throughout the night, with the periods of REM sleep becoming longer and longer, while the periods of deep delta become shorter and shorter. Finally, just before we awake in the morning at our regular time, REM is the longest, generating a dream sequence of perhaps twenty minutes' duration, while delta, or deep sleep, has almost completely diminished. We can look over at the alarm clock, however, just minutes before it goes off, and then go back to sleep. We might at that moment drop into one of those narrow but deep caverns of delta, a timeless void that seems like an eternity, only to be awakened minutes later by the bell.

One of the most interesting aspects of the hypnagogic state is our ability to make it conscious, to bring into the waking state what is normally just below the threshold of consciousness. People who record their own dreams essentially do this when they train themselves to wake up in the middle of the night to write their dreams down on paper. Often Carl Jung would wake up in the morning and see pages of dreams written out on the table beside his bed in his own handwriting, but have no memory of having written them.

Patricia Garfield, a California dream researcher, taught herself to write her dreams down in the dark while in a semi-conscious state, as she related in her work *Creative Dreaming*.[4] Her method was to hold a pen in her hand while she used one of her free fingers of the same hand to run along the edge of a 4-x-6 index card. Eventually, she learned how to write in straight lines in legible handwriting just by feel, even though the lights remained out. Before she mastered the art of doing this, however, she would often awaken in the morning and find part of her dream written in pen on her leg.

The psychoanalyst Herbert Silberer taught himself a method for eliciting what he called auto-symbolic phenomena in his search for the origin of symbolism within the normal personality.[5] Silberer trained himself to hover right at the edge of sleep for long periods so he could record the last conceptual thought in his mind just before he dropped off to sleep. Upon falling off, he would see the analytic thought suddenly visualized as a dream symbol, which he was also able to write down in this semi-conscious state.

The ability to make unconscious imagery conscious using sophisticated electronic equipment and computer analysis is now well established. The Voluntary Controls Project, originally founded by Elmer and Alyce Green at the Menninger Foundation in Topeka, Kansas, was eventually taken over by Dale Walters and others, who developed an exportable program to teach anyone how to translate cognitive thoughts into internal dream images while still remaining in the waking condition. The method used was to hook a recording electrode up to a subject's occipital lobe and take continuous EEG readings of beta, alpha, theta, and delta wave activity, which could be printed out over time on a computer. Subjects also wore earphones and had just two tones fed back into their ears. The two different tones told them when they were generating alpha and theta waves. Beta waves were filtered out, while delta waves were recorded on the computer, but no sound of their occurrence was fed back to the subject.

The training started with some relaxation exercises in a comfortable, darkened room. As soon as the subject's eyes were closed, the tone indicating alpha activity was heard. Since theta waves are very close in frequency to alpha, theta waves would also soon appear, but be heard by a slightly different tone. As the subject learned to differentiate between the two tones, he or she began to associate a mental image with the theta-wave tone. Within several hours, it was possible for the average subject, by simple concentration and relaxation, to learn how to translate common thoughts into dream images. Put another way, the feedback the subject received allowed him or her to experience dreaming while still awake. One would simply have a thought, which, as it bubbled up to the surface of consciousness, would be seen in the interior field of vision as a dream symbol or an extremely vivid mental image that was like a dream but experienced in a state of waking consciousness.

The significance of these experiments for healing is that we do have at hand workable methods to alter consciousness from its habitual attachment to material reality and to open that door into the unconscious by voluntarily going through the hypnagogic state. The process seems to involve not only transcending the bounds of the normal waking state to enter into these alternative realities, but also shifting the threshold of consciousness, so that what was before unconscious now becomes conscious. Dreaming, for instance, is normally a behavior of the unconscious, but to bring vivid mental imagery that is like a dream into the field of consciousness must necessarily widen the bounds of what we can now define as normal. What is normal, in other words, if we cannot also account for the immediate state of consciousness we are in when we look out and see a glass on the table or read these words or see a familiar face? Perception is not fixed but constantly in motion. The wonder is that we see anything consistently from one moment to the next at all.

I learned the techniques of the waking dream at a three-day seminar, during which the participants were asked to visualize their thoughts in a continuously flowing stream of mental images. It was extremely difficult for me to drive the eleven miles home each night on a six-lane highway, because every time I had a thought about the traffic, the scenery, or the car, I would experience it as a waking dream image. My solution to the problem was to drive exactly 55 miles per hour in the slow lane. This allowed me to drive safely on what could be called automatic pilot, while still enjoying the dream images passing through my mind, suggesting that there is a true change in perception, but that one can also adapt to it.

❧ The Hypnagogic State and Healing ❧

We have already alluded to the idea that, while the hypnagogic state is a doorway into the unconscious, it is also a domain of healing. Traditional depth-psychology has always maintained that unconscious contents can be revealed to consciousness through the interpretation of dream symbolism. Newer approaches in alternative medicine, however, suggest that, instead of demanding that unconscious contents find some acceptable way to be presented to rational consciousness, waking awareness can be taken out of the empirical state that is normally anchored in material reality and transported within to other possible states of consciousness, with important consequences for growth and healing of the whole person.

The technique for achieving this is guided mental imagery, as Jeanne Achterberg has suggested in her work *Imagery in Healing: Shamanism and Modern Medicine.*[6] This usually involves two people—say, a therapist and client—both starting in the normal waking state. The therapist takes the patient on an inward journey by verbalizing a stream of mental images, which the patient tries to visualize in his or her mind. This may have the effect of leading the patient into the hypnagogic state and then on into various altered dimensions of consciousness. While the therapist is the anchor of the experience, it is also common that the therapist enters into a light trance as well, but retains the capacity to bring the patient back to waking consciousness at any time.

Guided mental imagery has three principal components. The first of these is breath. Breath, of course, is life; we breathe automatically. Breathing reflects our immediate emotional state, becoming shallower the more tense we are and deeper the more relaxed. Yawning, for instance, means that we have inadvertently become so relaxed that the system is not getting enough oxygen, and a yawn fills the lungs quickly. Therefore, in many ways, breathing is a meter of the unconscious. At the same time, however, we also have the conscious ability to control our breathing. When we are tense, (and breathing is shallow), we can relax by consciously willing ourselves to take deep, full inhalations and long, slow exhalations. When we are tired, we can often rejuvenate ourselves by rapid-breathing exercises, which infuses the entire system with oxygen. As a function of both consciousness and the unconscious, breathing is an ideal mechanism for traversing from one state to the other.

One of the main functions of breath control is to induce a second component of mental imaging—deep muscle relaxation. In the most common exercises, a subject first places his or her body in a comfortable position, either sitting or lying down, and then consciousness is directed systematically from head to toe through the major muscle groups, tensing and then relaxing each set. Conscious attention can be directed to a particular spot, where deep, relaxed breathing can be applied to loosen and relax the muscles involved. The dead man's pose in yoga, for instance, designed for global relaxation of the entire frame, has the person lying on the floor, completely flat on his back, relaxed in every part of his body, feeling completely comfortable but increasingly heavy, and, as an added meditation to increase the effect, falling into the floor to the center of the earth.

Guided visualizations are the means by which a person's consciousness can be directed into specific sites of the body, to specific organs, and, it is theorized, even to specific cells. I have said that attention to breathing makes one conscious of a normally unconscious process. Consciousness of the lungs filling with air and then deflating is often more difficult to induce, but made easier when it is accompanied by the image of rising and falling waves, expanding and contracting spheres, or giant bellows. The exchange of gases in the lung—the absorption of oxygen and the release from the blood of carbon dioxide—might at first have to be imagined fully to develop some consciousness of it. Visualizing specific components of the blood is usually more complex. Cancer patients are taught to see macrophages, the body's natural killer cells, in a variety of different shapes and behaviors, all devouring the cancer cell. Indeed, one of the early exercises of mind-body medicine is to have the patient get in touch with his or her malignancy by conjuring up the mental image that best represents the form and shape of the tumor or the diseased cell. However dark and foreboding this image may be, it can be used to measure the patient's subjective sense of well-being over the course of therapy, because the image itself may change with any change, for better or worse, in the cancerous condition.

Mental visualizations can also be employed with deep muscle relaxation and breath control to allow awareness to enter into noncognitive states of consciousness. A patient suffering from repeated traumas or otherwise involved in a catastrophic illness can be guided to an internal place of peace and calm, where the physical body is at last at rest and the surface of consciousness has become quiet. The cognitive path to this place can be well marked, such as getting the person first to visualize a path over a mountain, down a valley, and into a giant meadow; the weather can be programmed for a cool refreshing breeze on a warm spring day; the air can be filled with the scents of favorite flowers, the taste of moisture, and the sound of birds in the distance. Physiological measures confirm the dramatic changes from the tension-filled body to a relaxed state. The patient can be instructed to return to this place of peace and rest each time the anxiety level from external forces begins to rise, or just for periodic moments of renewal.

Many more sophisticated visualizations exist in the traditions of Hindu yoga and Buddhist meditation that are thought to provide access to different levels of consciousness, making this example of the meadows and streams pale by comparison. The basic mechanism is still the same, however. Cognitive information held in the field of consciousness of one person (the meditation teacher or the therapist) is transmitted to the cognitive field of consciousness of another person (the student or patient), which then allows the student or patient to gain access to normally noncognitive states of awareness for purposes of growth and healing.

One of the simplest visualizations in yoga is an unadorned four-inch circle of a uniform color. The practitioner concentrates on this circle for so long that it becomes internalized; that is, when the person looks away from the circle, he or she can still mentally visualize it. Further stages include learning to call forth the circle at will in the internal mind's eye, or to otherwise manipulate the circle voluntarily within the sphere of one's own internal field of consciousness. All of this—like learning how to learn, as distinct from the content of what is learned—is to train one's mental capacities for the true purpose of yoga, which is the difficult work of transforming consciousness into a more purified condition.

One of the primary tools for this work is the three-fold technique of attention, concentration, and meditation. These three faculties are thought of as a single tool for grasping the internal reality of all objects of perception, as the ability to sustain awareness on an object so that attention remains calm but motionless. Attention to an object beyond a minute or so naturally develops into the experience of concentration. Concentration is sustained attention, but it is also the ability to quiet the mind and relax the breathing. In this relaxed, quiet, but uninterrupted looking, consciousness contemplates the object until, within the object, the mind is reflected back onto itself, like a mirror, as it were. Finally, absorption into the object occurs. Here, the perceiver and the object become yoked, seen in the same larger sphere of reality. In this condition, a person can look away and mentally model the object, once having internalized all its characteristics.

The goal of sustained concentration and absorption is to be able to see into the interior reality of all perceived objects of perception and, at the same time, to see the mind at work and to quiet its surface so that one can look into its depths. This is not the only kind of meditation, however. There is meditation on specific objects; there is meditation on specific spiritual ideas. There is meditation on the flow of events as they unfold before the view of our awareness. There is meditation to produce insight and to identify with the illuminating quality of consciousness, instead of merely with its contents. There is meditation on emptiness—a clear field with no thought, the ultimate nature of material existence, according to the Buddhists. Similarly in the Christian tradition, there is also meditation to realize Christ consciousness.

It seems reasonable to presume that whatever can be conceived can become an object of meditation. However, traditionally in both Asian and Western mystical traditions, meditation is a technique for taking one beyond the domain of conceptualization. To meditate on the experience of emptiness, for instance, is to use concepts to go to the farther reaches of discursive thought, and then launch into the domain of the non-rational, the non-sensory, and the non-conceptual. It has been my experience that, whatever the inward journey turns out to be, rational consciousness must first pass through the domain of mental imaging to get any further. The nature of these other states is always defined from that first step. To navigate beyond that point, one must turn to the language of poetry and myth.

6

Mythopoesis

Mythopoesis is a word used in the late-nineteenth century by the English classicist Frederick William Henry Myers to indicate a dynamic psychological relation between myths and poetic language.[1] Essentially, it means that poetry is a language that often grasps at the inexpressible, and, in good poetry, mythopoetic language succeeds in elevating personal experience to a level where an individual's reality is believed to unite with the experience of all humanity. At the same time, poetry may plunge us into depths of feeling where we have never gone before, or expand our horizon in other ways beyond the frontier of the known. Since myths typically function to unite people in a common experience of their culture, poetry and myths appeared to Myers to function in similar domains of interior experience within the individual, hence the term "mythopoesis."

Myers specifically applied the word to understanding how we can gain access to interior states of consciousness for the purpose of healing through the use of poetic and mythic imaging, an idea that subsequently had an important influence on the development of scientific psychotherapy, especially in the psychology of Carl Jung. Myers thought that, while we live habitually in the external world, experience also goes on at a mythic and poetic level of the subconscious. Illnesses, especially psychological troubles, were but the outward manifestation of inner turmoil. Healing could only come about by revealing the root at a deeper, inward level, not by treating merely the outward symptom.

Jung argued that creative visions of genius, visions of the religious, hallucinations of the insane, and myths, especially of primitive cultures, were related because all are emanations of deep structures in the unconscious, which he called archetypes.[2] While Jung spent his life treating mental illness, his primary focus was to create a psychology of individuation, meaning a psychology focused on the realization of an individual's highest potential. To effect such transformation, Jung, following Myers, believed that inner exploration meant dealing with these deep inward structures and drawing on the unique forms of energy that they possessed for creative rather than destructive purposes. His was not a psychology designed to cure neuroses, but an exploration of interior states in order to effect the overthrow of the ego by the self. Self-realization and not mere adjustment was the goal of personality development.

The practical conclusion we can draw from the work of Myers and Jung is that poetry and myths heal because they bring normally unconscious material into consciousness. We might at first think of ourselves sitting next to the bedside of a sick man, reading his favorite poetry aloud to him as a way to soothe and calm a troubled situation. To soothe and calm, we have already suggested, is to descend into depth. Think also of the origins of medicine in classical antiquity, when a person's power to heal was believed to be given by the gods, whose existence was told in myths and whose power was inferred constantly in the occurrence of both beneficial and terrible events. In the Greek temples of Asclepius, patients were conducted to sleeping chambers where they dreamt of their illness and their mode of recovery. Today, hope and expectation are harnessed when victims of a terrible disaster first see the sign of the red cross; even the smell and look of the dispensary can suggest to the sick man that he is in the presence of a power greater than himself—that of science—and that, by coming into this presence, his suffering will be lightened. Here again is Herbert Benson's idea of remembered wellness, the ability of the body through a long chain of genetic memories to return to health.

From a psychological standpoint, I suggest that the answer to how symbols heal lies in the amount of psychic energy words or pictures contain in terms of their meaning for the individuals who are articulating or receiving them. Ideas have power, especially when they give us knowledge that we can use to understand the course of events. This is true of both the internal and external environment, except that the information is applied in radically different ways depending on whether we are talking about the outward connection between consciousness and material objects or the internal process of personality transformation.

As I have already said, the basic premise of scientific psychology is that there is only one reality—the physical and the material. Consequently, according to this view, the true psychological domain is based on information that comes in through the senses that can be discriminated by consciousness through objective measurement and then rationally ordered into proper categories for immediate reaction or storage and retrieval. The domain of mental imagery, on the other hand, is considered to be fictitious. Here, the scientists say, is the source of fantasy, superstition, the not-real.

But if one has experienced an opening of the internal sense and has developed familiar commerce with interior realities, then episodes in which the unconscious is made conscious become commonplace, and the opening of the threshold of consciousness may be a regular, daily, even hourly, event. For the psychologist, meaning is derived only from accuracy of physical measurements, which permits us to have greater control over the external environment. In the process of self-knowledge, as in self-healing, however, transmuting the abstract idea into a mental image is the primary means by which consciousness learns to communicate with nonconscious states of awareness.

A scientific measurement may have more than one meaning, but the goal is to be able to specify as accurately as possible the precise meaning of a term. In the process of interior exploration, however, the more meanings a term has the greater its energic power. This is the inherent difference between signs and symbols. A sign means just one thing—clouds, wind, and one-hundred-percent humidity mean bad weather; a stop sign at an intersection means to come to a complete halt; a green light means to proceed. A symbol, on the other hand, means that the image or idea before you stands for something else, either literally or suggestively. A police badge is a symbol of authority. Robes are a symbol of the judiciary or of a religious person. In Western culture, a white lab coat and small black bag are symbols of the physician; meanwhile, physicians themselves symbolize their art by the caduceus, or winged snake wrapped around a sword. Thus, a sign has a limited meaning in order to convey a single purpose, while a symbol is a representation of a larger and more all encompassing domain of experience.

But symbols also have a visionary aspect. Certain symbols carry spiritual meaning; they transport us from the domain of everyday existence into the realm of a more purified state of consciousness. It is in such states that the healing of the spirit takes place. It is true that our world is full of symbols, most of them given meaning by others who transmit to us what our family, our clan, or our culture believes is important. But there is a different kind of symbol that has to do with personal transformation. These are internal symbols that emerge within our field of awareness as a result of interior exploration. They are clues to the level of personality development that a person has attained; they are guideposts that point the way on the road to self-realization, and they are also treasured memories of the interior places we have been.

The type of imagery I am taking about I call symbols of personal destiny. These are particularly vivid impressions of no particular significance to anyone else except the individual who has them. Yet at the same time they are keys to the very core of who we are. Their discovery provides a kind of map to the path we have taken in our personal development. Their representation is an extraordinarily personal task that gives us a way to navigate around in the unconscious when we call such symbols forth. At the same time, they are a bridge between different states of consciousness that feed into the normal waking state.

As a college student stuck during a winter vacation in upstate Pennsylvania, I had the opportunity to immerse myself in a small-town library in collections of ethnographic literature about various American Indian tribes. I read that, when a Chippewa Indian boy ate his meals, there was always a bowl of coal on the table that no one would acknowledge. All attempts to ask why the bowl was there went unanswered, until one day the boy would realize that he must choose the bowl of coal over the bowl of food. According to the custom of the Chippewa, the boy was then taken by the elders into the wilderness to fast for a vision that would determine his place in the tribe's social structure. A similar vision quest was performed among the American Plains Indians, who painted the boy's vision on a shield of animal hide and hung it outside his lodge for everyone to see into his unique spiritual reality.[3]

The symbols painted on the shield may have had significance in the tribe's myths; but, for the boy, they told the story of his individual journey, of his personal destiny. They also depict his path from the ignorance of waking consciousness attached to material reality to higher and more self-actualized states of consciousness. They may repeat themselves over time, or they may be stepping stones to other collections of symbols that supersede them and mark yet another level or stage of personal development. They may be entirely pedestrian and so common that they repeat themselves over and over from person to person; or they may be unique to the individual.

Likewise, everyone of us collects such symbols throughout the course of a lifetime. I have a dream image of my earliest memory, for instance. I say this because in my attempt to recover my earliest memories, a task which I return to periodically, I could not tell whether the earliest image I have occurred in waking reality or in a dream. I remember a particularly vivid nightmare when I was young, the impression of which has stayed with me to this day. I carry that dream now as more of an enigma—that the impression has embedded within it some secret I have to find, some hidden meaning that is a clue to my further growth.

I have described my early vision of Jesus on the cross. This I believe is another important symbol in the evolution of my personal destiny. I have a favorite color, and I become attached periodically to certain numbers. There are certain mystical and contemplative places I seem to return to again and again over the course of my life. There are certain pictures and certain motifs that seem to recur over and over again, certain kinds of people I am always called upon to interact with, certain themes that characterize my struggle to understand reality. All of these in the larger perspective are representative of the course my life has taken and are symbolic representations of my personal destiny.

After I had spent eight years studying the language, religion, and philosophy of India, one of my friends asked me to try an experiment: the next time I was in one of the giant used book stores in the town in which I lived, I should find the *National Geographic* for the month and year I was born. I found the issue, and there was a special sixteen-page section on the life and culture of Pakistan, which had once been a part of British India. I thought that surely this was a sign of the star I was born under. No one else would think so, however. To anyone else, only coincidence connected the content of my life with the content of the magazine. Nevertheless, despite logic, despite science, despite reason, in our heart of hearts, deep inside of us, when such synchronous events occur, we are sure that, in the larger course of our life, we have taken the right path, however insignificant the episodes may seem to others. This is because, as William Faulkner once pointed out, we never know when a person is really open, when he or she is most vulnerable to the slightest change in our tone of voice, when mere innuendo creates a slight that wounds us or that inspires a guiding impression that is seared into the unconscious for a lifetime.

As I interpret him, Swedenborg maintained that, when there is an opening of the internal spiritual sense, an influx of the Divine occurs that transforms even the most mundane of events. We then see the correspondence of all aspects of the natural world with those of the spiritual. I suppose he would say that such synchronous events as the discovery of the parallelism of the contents of that *National Geographic* with events in my own life represented an example of the harmonization of our interiors with our exteriors. The message for me had already registered nonverbally, at a level far deeper than words. Divine providence was the term Swedenborg used; Jung called it synchronicity.[4]

This is also to say that symbols become visionary when they become numinous. For example, a cross to the Christian world stands for the crucifixion; but it could also call forth a host of other images about religious teachings, charismatic individuals one has met, or personal inward experiences that one has had. In the case of personal symbols, however, the depth of meaning is directly proportional to the amount of illumination we receive on the way.

I have often wondered if, in a room full of people, it might be possible to see revealed all at once each individually inspired system of personal mythology. I imagined, as Joseph Campbell already knew, that there was a map of the world somewhere in which not the physical boundaries of countries were depicted, but the mythological systems unique to that culture. If there were such a map, certainly we would then have before us the picture of a world mythology—the contribution that each culture makes toward an archetypal vision of world consciousness. I have inevitably found that a knowledge of the mythology of a particular culture goes a long way toward comprehending the worldview of that culture, the conceptions of personality and consciousness unique to that culture, and that unnameable something that reflects unique tastes, moods, and experiential ways of being. Likewise, a deep understanding emerges on discovering the unique symbols of destiny that comprise the worldview of a single individual or that represent the bond in a dyadic relationship, family, or clan.

This is the great conundrum—what is the relation of the individual to the collective? What is the relation between the particular and the universal? I take an example from a close friend and Jungian analyst, who experienced a dream vision, which occurred at the moment of a major stroke that permanently paralyzed him. It comes from what the two of us have humorously called "The Annals of Jim Hall's Strangest Experiences." My friend, Dr. James Hall, first gives his account and then I give my analysis. Hall writes:

As near as I can pinpoint it, this dream/vision occurred about the time of my brainstem stroke in early 1991. I don't know whether to call it a dream or a vision.

I was drowning in a vaporous ocean. There was a large crouching muscular male figure on the beach. I desperately asked for help, but seemed to communicate by telepathy. I asked to be allowed to live out my life with my wife, Suzanne. The figure did not move, but suddenly I knew that I would live thirty more years, to age 87. The sequence, whatever it was, vanished. My next memory was of waking up virtually quadriplegic in an intensive-care unit.

Fr. Morello, my priest-friend, immediately thought the crouching figure might be Jesus, but it was unlike any representation I have ever seen. In my memory the figure has taken on more the form of a gladiator, but I think that is retrospective. Might it have been the Self?[5]

In my own analysis of Jim's experience, I felt that the figure was his spirit-body—the ideal form of the physical, turning around for one last look before taking a permanent exit. In that split second, Jim's psyche asked, "Will I live or die?" and the answer was given by the self—that greater and more enduring product of individuation—which was not the crouching muscular figure (the verbs he used suggest this, as the answer did not come necessarily from the figure)—he would live on to 87, but (flash, freeze-frame—next moment, consciousness, waking up a quadriplegic in the ICU) not in that spirit-body, as the spirit figure had departed after its last look.

While this was quite a little drama, I had to admit that I was merely hallucinating on the meaning of my friend's vision. After all, Jung himself had said that there is no interpretation of the dream apart from the dreamer. It would take Jim's own free associations on the different symbols of the dream to unlock the secrets they contain for him.

One can imagine what a terrible experience that this must have been for Jim. His ability to cast it into a visionary and mythic perspective, however, allows the traumatic event to serve as a springboard for further self-analysis and philosophical questioning, as a source of healing rather than as a source of despair and self-destruction. By such means, we are once again confronted with the mythic and poetic imperative. We need poetry to feed the life of the soul, and we need to be guided by living myths if spiritual growth and transformation are to take place.

7

Heaven and Hell

Wwhat are the realms of heaven and hell but states
of our own interior consciousness? Phenomenologically, if the external, natural world is but
an emanation of the higher, deeper, and all-encompass-
ing domain of the spirit, and if this domain is made manifest in the external world through human experience,
then surely all conceptions of heaven and hell are states
of our own interior consciousness projected outward.
This is my interpretation of Swedenborg's psychology;
and with additional modifications, it has close similarities
to the Jamesian view, the Jungian view, the view of
Joseph Campbell, the Sufi view, and the view held by the
major Hindu and Buddhist schools, among others.

The idea that heaven and hell refer to our own interior states is not new. The myth of Demeter and
Persephone as it appears in different forms suggests

more than simply the origin of the seasons. The basic story recounts how Persephone was abducted and taken to the netherworld. She was rescued when her mother, Demeter, pleaded with the gods and struck a deal that would return the daughter to her family, but all she could get was half the year. Hence, the months when Persephone must return to Hades we know as fall and winter. Her emergence from the netherworld heralds the months of spring and summer.

A psychological meaning of the same myth might suggest that renewal in personality takes place by a periodic immersion into domains of the unconscious. But this, however, is only an interpretation. At one point in the not-too-distant past, there was an exchange between the Hindu yogi Sri Auribindo Ghose and the French scholar Louis Renou.[1] Auribindo maintained that the hymns of the Vedas, his native scriptures, were actually metaphors about personality transformation. The great Renou proclaimed that this was preposterous, since the evidence was clear that the texts were nothing more than hymns to nature, to the dawn, the sky, and the earth. Auribindo retorted that he was puzzled about how the interpretation of a foreigner could somehow be put forward as more accurate than the native to whom the myths actually belonged. There is no record of Renou's response.

If we take Auribindo's point of view, works such as John Bunyan's *Pilgrims Progress* and Dante's *Inferno* can be seen as maps of these interior states. Researchers at the turn of the last century, such as F. W. H. Myers, believed that, through their investigation of mediumistic trance states, they had identified a spectrum of internal states of consciousness ranging from the psychopathic to the transcendent. Now various scholars of mysticism such as Mircea Eliade, Robert Forman, and Huston

Smith and transpersonal psychologists such as Charles Tart and Stanislav Grof have written extensively on such a spectrum, meanwhile drawing heavily from the world's religious traditions.[2]

Swedenborg had made the same point as early as 1758, in his work *Heaven and Hell*. According to the account Swedenborg left of his own revelation, God had spoken to him through the angels and told him that, with the opening of the internal spiritual sense, he should commence writing down the true but hidden meaning of the books of the Bible. Subsequently, as Swedenborg pursued this task, he would regularly turn within and, in communication with the angels, be conducted through the various domains of heaven and hell. He first recorded his observations in his diaries—what became known as the *Spiritual Diaries* (published posthumously)—and later compiled his thoughts and visions in the more formal *Heaven and Hell*.

In *Heaven and Hell*, Swedenborg maintained that the most fundamental fact of heaven is that it was the highest, best, and most profound vision of God, a vision even beyond all conception. By this he meant that everything that was of the Divine—everything that was good and true: all peace, love, charity, and faith; and all of the finest and best and highest characteristics of what it means to be human—is heaven. He envisioned heaven as an infinite number of different societies, large and small, peopled by angels who were the unique representations of the personalities of all who had ever lived. Moreover, there were different types of heaven, each arranged in terms of their proximity to God—the celestial sphere is nearest, while the spiritual sphere comes next. Then there is the domain of the merely natural. There are also three different degrees of heaven depending on what was outermost, innermost, and in-between. These are the different domains leading from the soul, which is the individual's own spirit, down finally to the thoughts and affections of the rational person and the physical body as we think it exists in the natural world. As a higher spiritual state of consciousness, the heavenly domains and their different societies represent in their totality the Lord, which Swedenborg characterized as the Grand Man, because of the representation of the Lord in all that was divinely human.

Further, there is a middle condition, half way between heaven and hell, which Swedenborg conceived as the domain of spirits. This is an intermediate state, into which the person enters just after death, and which represents the condition of a person's interiors. To the extent that a person was made up of good and truth, he or she goes on to heaven; and to the extent that he or she was made up of evils and falsities, the spirit goes on to the hells. The conjunction with one or the other is made in this middle state. Swedenborg describes it in *Heaven and Hell*:

> The world of spirits appears like a valley between mountains and rocks, with here and there windings and elevations. The gates and doors to the heavenly societies are not seen, except by those who are prepared for heaven, nor are they found by others; to every society there is one entrance from the world of spirits, and then one way, branching in the ascent into several. Neither are the gates and doors to the hells seen, except by those who are about to enter, to whom they are then opened; and when they are opened, there appear caverns dusky and as if sooty, tending obliquely down toward the deep, where again there are many

doors. Through these caverns are exhaled nauseous and fetid stenches which good spirits flee from, because they have an aversion to them, but which evil spirits seek for, because they are their delights.[3]

Swedenborg also said that all who are in hell are ruled by fears, a plainly psychological statement. Further, there is not one devil who presides over hell, but many hells inhabited by humans who delighted in evils and falsities in the natural world, who each have become the devil ruling the place they are in. Hell is the origin of evils, which are states of a man's own consciousness. God does not cast us down into hell. Rather, he is always drawing us to himself. We, however, by the way we have lived, by shunning good and doing evil, create states of consciousness full of suffering and pain that are directly opposite from that of heaven. For this reason, Swedenborg believed that there are as many societies in hell as there are in heaven, which are completely opposite in composition and effect. The hells are the realms of perpetual punishments because of self-love and because we cling to the idea that the merely material world is all there is to reality.

In a more modern context, following the interior meaning of the kind of spiritual psychology we are discussing, one could say that hell is described in *The Diagnostic and Statistical Manual of Mental Disorders* (DSM), used by psychiatrists, psychologists, and insurance companies to classify a patient's symptoms according to the categories of major and minor mental illness.[4] Here we have an almost complete compendium of human suffering. The psychoneuroses—character problems, thought and mood disorders, dysfunctions of personality, obsessions and compulsions—and the major psychoses—

paranoia, manic-depression, and schizophrenia—are all described. Most of the preferred explanations for how these disorders develop or should be treated are based on scientific experiments and inferential theory and are considered largely biological or genetic in origin. Despite the thickness of the DSM, its excessive weight, and its command as an authoritative statement, the explanations it contains remain only tentative, not only subject to revision based on new scientific information, but also susceptible to being completely overthrown by practitioners who do not believe in the biological basis of mental illness.

The most interesting element absent from the descriptions of mental illness in the DSM is the patient's own phenomenological understanding of a particular condition. There are no first-person accounts of what patients said about the course of their illnesses; there are no analyses of the symbolic content of someone's mental ideation; there are no stories of real, live people.

We can only imagine what such a phenomenological description of a disorder might be like. Depression is an example of an illness that has a familiar phenomenological course. There are extraordinarily severe and chronic instances of severe depression that are chemical, have no known cause, but seem to come from deeply within. These are the endogenous forms. There is also reactive depression, which is usually temporary and comes from the body's natural reaction to trauma and loss. Millions of people experience this latter type at some time over the course of their lives. Reactive depression has a natural cycle of shock, numbness, anger, and then recovery. Sometimes it is treated with medication and psychotherapy, sometimes just with social support, sometimes with nothing. Even so, the person eventually recovers some sense of normalcy

Within the framework of a psychology of inner experience, no more common example exists of the correspondence between a state of consciousness and the domain of the infernal than the experience of depression. As everyone knows who has experienced it, depression is hell. From the standpoint of personal phenomenology, from the standpoint of the experience of the person, all objective attempts to describe this condition, be they medical, psychological, or literary, do not come close to the feeling that, in the midst of it, the sufferer has found the lowest, darkest, and most forgotten place of all humanity.

The initial phase of a reactive depression can be a psychic explosion. We may experience grief, a sense of loss, isolation, and psychological pain beyond anything we thought bearable, but which now seems to go on forever. The orderliness of everything formerly known, the sense of familiarity, the security that comes from routine, all disappear in an instant. This despondency may occur because we have lost a lifelong companion. Or a child has been taken away, or a limb is gone, or we can no longer see. Perhaps our mental capacities are diminished. Or perhaps we are mired in an unresolvable emotional conflict, which shows every sign of being a permanent but intolerable condition. There are many sources of a depressive episode, but they all agree in that they are a natural and human reaction to something that has happened.

In the second phase comes numbness. The world becomes completely flat. We may go on for seemingly indefinite periods and feel incapable of expressing any kind of emotion, as if encased in a gigantic envelope, as if surrounded by a gel that prevents anything from getting in to offer comfort or getting out to make contact with the external world. And yet, while seemingly robbed of all emotion, in the very next instant, we may burst into tears, may be seized by a sense of grief, which all of a sudden wells up from the unconscious like a giant wave, which picks us up and pitches us down. There, we are held, agonizing internally, until we are released by some equally unknown force. Sometimes if we just give ourselves up to this overwhelming grief, it disappears in an instant. At other times, there is nothing we can do but try to survive until it passes again into the unconscious.

Likewise the elicitation of emotion may come about from an external source. We may be watching a movie, when suddenly we are stirred by some theme, the heroism of a mother, the self-sacrifice of the leading man, the intense suffering of a whole group of people subjected to some injustice. And as these feelings are stirred for others in the artificial environment of the theater, suddenly, we are confronted with our own pain. We become overwhelmed, not by the theme of the movie, but by the realization that our numbness was protecting us from how deeply hurt we still feel within ourselves, for we have not yet healed.

In this numbness there is also a profound sense of isolation. We look out onto the world and see people going about their business, trying to make a living, trying to survive, trying at least to be as average as possible. But we seem to look at them over a great chasm. We may be standing right next to someone else, yet, within us, we feel we must be millions of miles apart. We speak to them and they answer, yet we feel we are calling out over a great distance. We may feel that it takes us forever to reach them in order to say a single word, the chasm we are experiencing at that moment may feel so great. We may even feel that the effort to bridge the apparently unbridgeable, just to say a single word to them, is too great, so we remain encased in our silence, and the chance to speak passes out of our reach.

During such times, we are also seized with an apparently unending sense of hopelessness and despair. We are in constant pain, which has no boundaries. Our thoughts are negative, dark, and foreboding. Our sense of isolation feels so complete that there seems no point to anything. No point to getting up in the morning, so we are always late. No point to looking after our appearance, so our clothes do not get cleaned. No point in contacting anyone, so we stay in for days or weeks at a time. No point to preparing a decent meal, so we begin loosing weight; or, at the other extreme, fall into a pathological kind of snacking. The weight of the world seems upon us; the well of despair seems cavernous. Often, we cannot find a reason for anything. All we know is that we cannot bear these feelings, yet we must continue to endure them. This is our Dark Night of the Soul.

Then, after numbness, comes anger. We may become angry at the mailman for getting the mail wet. We may be angry at the way the toaster is not working. We may become angry at abstract circumstances, such as the stupidity of the government or the insensitivity of strangers toward each other. In all of these cases, there may or may not be some legitimate cause for directing our feelings at a particular object or circumstance. In most cases, we are expressing something beneath the surface; these things are our targets, but we are projecting something common onto all of them.

Our reaction may alarm people who get near us, but it is not simply repressed rage. After all, this is a healthy kind of anger, because it is the first genuine expression of a human emotion to burst forth above the surface of the unconscious, the first emotion that mitigates our abject despair. It represents not repressed feelings, but free air. We are finally coming back to the land of the living. And while we may seem angry against the world, we are also angry with ourselves. It is paradoxical anger because we are mad at ourselves for being gone for so long—for being lost within. We might not be pleasant to be around, but something positive is definitely happening.

Here we have the chance for some remarkable opportunities. Instead of just railing against the world, we can become fighters for some cause. We can dedicate ourselves to something outside ourselves that our depression has at last allowed us to see. We might address some injustice, provide some service, anything that helps us to reach out further beyond ourselves. A recovering breast cancer patient may start a support group. A mother whose daughter died in a car crash might join a chapter of Mothers against Drunk Driving. A father who lost his son might join Big Brothers. A recovered mental patient might assist in the rights of other patients.

Or we might also just do nothing. We might not go out and try to change the world. Still, in myriad small ways, we find the means to rededicate ourselves to life. We might at last clean up where we live, throw out old things, rehang the pictures, go somewhere we have never gone before, get more vocal, or just start speaking differently than we had in the past. The main thing is that we now feel different, better, less numb. And, with this sense of feeling better often comes a pervasive feeling of gratitude, a point we shall elaborate shortly.

During such times, when we are able again to speak to the world, it also helps to be pleasantly superficial. To engage in chitchat now seems like a miracle to someone who only months or weeks before could not even bring him- or herself to speak. To be able to respond to the sound of voices, instead of just hearing them across the great chasm of some inward prison, to be able to talk without any hidden motives, to be able to listen, but now with a sense of gratitude that the other person talking could not possibly imagine, these are the signs of recovery.

Of course, in these moments, we also discover that we are not quite yet well. This can occur when pleasantly superficial conversation turns to more serious matters. When someone asks, "How are you?" you quickly learn not to be blunt and bare the naked truth. The proper response is "I'm fine; how are you?"—not "Well, to tell you the truth, my father just died, I lost my job, my wife has just filed for divorce, and I just declared bankruptcy; but other than that, I'm doing all right." As the Chinese Taoists say, one's *chi*, or spirit, is still burning white-hot just below the surface, while everything seems calm above. It is not uncommon for the person asking you how you are to be burnt to a crisp, if all of the sudden for some reason, the curtain on the unconscious is raised, and you show them what is really happening. Such courtesy in protecting others from the white heat of our own *chi* is the true mark of a person on the road to recovery.

Recovery means that one has emerged from the confines of private suffering and realized that what has happened to him or her is an opportunity now to see in a new way the suffering of others—just as the grieving woman did in the Buddhist tale recounted earlier. Private pain becomes the realization of universal emotion—that I have suffered now allows me to more deeply appreciate the fact that all people suffer. A mother who has lost her child goes through her own private grieving period for what she has lost. But then after a time, her mourning is over and she emerges into the world again, now taking her place along with all the mothers who have lost their children. Her return makes her not only more sensitive to the plight of other mothers, but also more wise, in that her loss which can never be recovered gives her a new way to look at the world. In this way, she is able to retake her place in the flow of humanity. Thus it is, to emerge from one of the states of hell.

But now turn to the description of the various stages leading to heaven. Heaven has many descriptions. Take the one presented by the Sufis, who represent the mystical wing of Islam. The path, they say, is nothing less than love (*'ishq* or *mahabba*). Love, of course, has many moods and degrees; but, in its mystical classification according to the Persian Sufis, love is understood in the context of a mystical psychology of stages or stations of attainment, where the greatest emphasis is placed on love as the transcendence of the self—love aspiring to union with God.

Following the description given by Ruzbihan Baqli, in his Persian text, *The Jasmine of the Lovers*, we have the mystical ascent to perfect love in twelve stations.[5] The first is servanthood, or preparation through fasting, prayer, silence and the remembrance of God. The second is the practice of sainthood, which involves repentance, piety, and asceticism. The third is meditation, the control of random thoughts so that one can see into one's own true nature. The fourth is fear, by which is meant a purifying fire that instills the manners of the prophets. The fifth is hope, which is the antidote for fear. The sixth is finding, which refers to encountering the nearness of the beloved. The seventh is certainty, an experience beyond the mere unshakable faith of the ordinary person, one that is rather a direct perception of divine attributes in the heart. The eighth is nearness, meaning ascent to the divine presence in an increasingly intensive transcendence. The ninth is the unveiling; here love and beauty are joined in the soul to reveal divine lordship. The tenth is witnessing, which refers to the act of seeing in states of both sobriety and intoxication. The eleventh is love proper, referring not just to a vision of beauty in creation, but to a vision of love in its procreated state, a vision of its state as a spirit not veiled in any human characteristics, where the divine beloved is encountered without any intervening medium; it is a vision of the unimpeded love for God in eternity. Here the lover is transformed into the mirror of God, so that whoever looks upon the lover in turn becomes a lover of God. The twelfth and final stage is longing, a divine unity where the distinction between love and longing becomes paradoxical, a fire that burns away all thoughts, desires, and veils from the heart. There is only God, love, lover, and beloved. This is heaven as a state of highest consciousness.

8

The Speech of Angels

S wedenborg once wrote, "The thoughts of angels were perceived as rainbows."[1] An arch rationalist could not possibly believe this statement, first because it sounds like pure fantasy, but, more disturbingly, because it implies the reality of angelic beings. But Swedenborg, as Ralph Waldo Emerson, Charles Sanders Peirce, and William James did later, had a wider definition of reason than does the arch rationalist. In his arguments about the nature of psychological reality, Swedenborg appropriated intuition in service of reason. Logic is informed by insight, not separated from it. Or put more succinctly, Swedenborg maintained that spiritual consciousness is not a byproduct or a tributary; rather, it is the source of all discursive knowledge. Normally, we have been taught to think that anything presented to the logical mind has to come in the form of a concrete fact, which rational consciousness then registers as an abstraction, while the language of the spirit is all metaphor and imagery—that is, the product of our imagination.

Ah, but if the rationalist only knew what imagination really is! Imagery, as we have said, is the doorway into the unconscious. Metaphor is the way rational consciousness is permitted to communicate with domains beyond itself. Communication is all nonverbal, for it has quite transcended language. So when Swedenborg conversed in rainbows, it was color and energy absorbed by the spirit, not merely words heard by the anatomical ear.

The matter of angels, however, is more problematic. Swedenborg said angels are souls of the dead, who live in heaven in angelic form. There are also souls who exist as spirits in the intermediary plane—the world of spirits described in the preceding chapter—not having decided yet which affinities to associate with and hence whether they would live for eternity in the realms of the heavens or the hells.

Jung, on the other hand, described the perception of spirit entities within us as fragments of our own personality. In their most primitive form, we see them as alienated parts of ourselves. They are the things we see about ourselves which we deny, the painful realities of who we are as others see us when we are most blind to the elements of our own character. They are our most dreaded foibles—hidden from our own view but glaringly there for everyone else to see.

There was a musician I once knew, a tuba player in an orchestra, who would always sidle up to the youngest and prettiest women musicians who were sitting in their seats practicing. Thinking himself suave and debonair, he intended to engage them in conversation. As he approached them, however, he always stuck his hips out so that they protruded nearest to them, but he remained completely unconscious of this behavior. As a result, the women in the orchestra referred to him among themselves as "hips first"; and, after a while, the phrase became a clandestine source of humor throughout the entire community of musicians. Meanwhile, he never caught on.

Similarly, when Swedenborg's *Journal of Dreams*, originally composed in Swedish, was first published in English, some ministers of the New Church were in a quandary about the frank and candid descriptions of images that had obvious sexual overtones. They determined, as a matter of propriety, to put those parts in Latin, which, of course, only made them easier to find, once the educated got their first look at the book.

The point is that we often repress what we deny about ourselves; at the same time, however, what we repress tends unconsciously to control us. But according to Jung, our worst faults are not bad or ugly, just underdeveloped parts of our personality. They are, in fact, he also said, guardians to the inner door. They are the barriers that prevent us from entering further into the unconscious because we may not yet be prepared. We may have other work to do first before we can enter that door. In any case, as long as we see them in their most fearful aspect, they shroud the interior domain and make it invisible to waking vision.

But once we see the disparate parts of ourselves for what they are, their nature becomes transparent. To deal with them unflinchingly, to stand by our weaknesses and acknowledge them, is to say that, while they may be bigger than the scope of our interior sight at this moment, they cannot exert blind control over us because we recognize them, even if we do not actually control them,

Moreover, they are no longer the means by which others can gain control over our lives.

Paradoxically, when we confront the undeveloped aspects of our personality, when we face our greatest fears, we find in them the conditions needed to take the next step. What were before the guardians of the inner door now become guides or allies.

Once I had to move unexpectedly in mid-winter. Additionally, the event looked like it was going to happen under a variety of unfortunate circumstances. First of all, I had a bad case of the flu. Second, moving day was upon me, and I still had not found another place to live. Third, the truck rental company said it had no large trucks available, although I could rent the smallest truck it had. The only problem was that I had to bring the truck back at the end of each day and fill out new paper work each time, because I could rent the truck only one day at a time. Fourth, I had no idea how I was going to move all my belongings by myself.

When the fateful day came, I was completely numb. I knew I had an extraordinary number of things to do, but I could do none of them. I felt immobilized, unable to lift a finger. Actually, I was suffering from a paralysis of the will—a common enough symptom under traumatic circumstances. Having located a place to move my belongings only the day before, I faced moving day, a day that was freezing cold and drizzly. I was still in shock.

As I stood there surveying the immensity of the task before me, someone whom I did not actually know very well, but who had heard that I might need some help moving, showed up with a large number of cardboard boxes and packing tape. A young woman who had heard I was sick then appeared, promising at least to carry the small things. Next came a teenager who had heard from one of my friends that there might be a job available carrying the big items. Finally, a young man in his early twenties arrived unexpectedly. He had just come into town from Chicago and heard from his parents that I was moving. Five years earlier, I had helped him as a teenager during an acute drug crisis and then given him a temporary job helping me move into the place I was now vacating. When the young man heard that I was moving again, but under difficult circumstances, he rushed over to offer his help. Using only the smallest of the rental trucks available, I was moved to my new location by the end of the day.

The point of this story is that, at those moments of personal destiny, in this case my hour of greatest need, circumstances sometimes conspire to deliver what is required. At such moments, angelic beings appear, in this case, serendipitously disguised as movers, and they help guide us to an entirely new state of consciousness. This is what Jung meant when he said that, if a man is sitting in his own home alone and has the right thought, he will be heard a thousand miles away. Similarly, while we are required to take the inward journey by ourselves, once we have actually embarked in that quest, soon, Jung also said, unknown friends will appear.

Another manifestation of the angelic in inward experience is the phenomenon of self-witnessing. In psychiatry, this is considered pathological, and the patient is referred to as having what is called ideas of reference, such as when someone speaks of him- or herself in the third person. Such an experience is thought to be self-alienation. As a religious phenomenon, however, self-witnessing is an important stage in the process of self-realization. In the self-psychology of Vedanta, for instance, the individualized sense of personal identity (*jiva* or *citta*) thinks, speaks, and acts out in the material world, while the spiritual self (*atman*), the supreme state of consciousness within, looks on, unaffected by the karmic activities of the material self.[2] Similarly, as I have said, William James posited that we are a conglomeration of discrete selves—biological, material, and social, with an internal spiritual self that witnesses the activities of the other ones.

But who or what is looking down on us, if we are not the names, the addresses, the possessions, even the physical bodies we have been trained to call ourselves all this time? Is it in that higher self that we lose our personal identity, and in that more open spiritual state receive communications from angelic beings? From the Divine itself? I will save such a discussion for a later chapter. My only point here is that, in self-witnessing, I believe that we come in contact with a higher part of ourselves, where personal identity tends to melt into something greater, deeper, wider and more encompassing than what we have known before.

At one point in my earlier life when I was a student and would sometimes stay up for several days intensely reading my books, I had such a visionary look into what I call the book of my personal destiny. It was around dawn of the second or third day I had been at my studies. I was simultaneously tired from and excited about what I was working on, so I could neither sleep in the normal sense, nor continue to concentrate on the task of reading. Instead, probably because I was not particularly occupied with anything at the moment, I drifted into a kind of reverie. I saw myself sitting on the side of the bed reading a large book. The pages seemed to be transparent, somewhat like the transparent layovers in a high-school biology book that show the systems of a frog in different colors, where on one page is the musculature system, on another the circulatory system, on another the nerves, and so on. The difference was that on each page in this book there was a picture of my own face. As I leafed through the pages, one after another, face after face, I saw my destiny pass before me—all the different faces that I was or had been—something on the order of a pictorial review of my life. When I awoke, I felt as if I had seen something important, much as if I had just made a summary of discrete information and collected everything into a series of pictures that pointed in a now more-definite direction. I cannot at this time remember the end of the book, only that I was intensely in that present moment. I do remember, however, the fragment of a vision of myself in the bathroom mirror. Although I was then in my early twenties, I saw myself in middle age—much different than I actually look now, because it seems to me that it was an idealized conception of how I might look in the future. I do remember, however, that it was a picture of perfect health. The question of who or what is healed was not answered by this experience. I did suspect, however, that what we take for separate entities within are, in reality, different parts of the same self.

Yet what is that self at its farthest reaches? To what extent are we autonomous, and to what extent do we participate in the psychic reality of others? Is it not possible to make contact with others from within? I suppose this is what Swedenborg meant when he referred to the marriage of souls. It certainly helps to explain who our guardian angels might be. From a mythopoetic standpoint, guardian angels are the spirits of others that envelop us—our parents, brothers and sisters, closest friends; the haunting quality of our mates, made known to us especially in moments of absence from them; they are the souls of our children, of the mentors in our life, and of our ancestors. Their presence gives meaning to the idea that each of us lives surrounded by the souls of others. As each parent dies, we see more clearly our own mortality; they are all that stands between us and our own grave—a realization that is not really morbid, only the wisdom that comes from age and experience.

When the suicide victim, who believed that no one in the world loved him, is dead, his body is delivered to the waiting hands of relatives, from whom he was only estranged. When we have lost our partner or our mate, we are left exposed to the vicissitudes of the world because we are, even if only temporarily, without the immediate protection of other souls. We become vulnerable, and unwanted influences may then more freely intrude. This is the symbolic reason that a father traditionally gives his daughter away in marriage to the new son-in-law. She is passed from under the protection of one soul to another without interruption. In the chaos of today, however, the ideal is no longer always possible, so individuals must learn how to make their own way, or else invent new sacraments commensurate with new definitions of the family. A family might not only exist by ties of blood. There could be new configurations, presided over by surrogate mothers and fathers who become, as necessity and love call them, spontaneous guardian angels of the young.

Other types of angelic beings might be the few people we have met throughout the course of our lives whom we may call our mentors or guides. These are people who may or may not teach us something specific, but who accept who we are wholeheartedly and without question. Each one of us can count such beings on the fingers of one hand, for it seems that we are blessed with no more than a few of such people in a single lifetime.

I can remember my tenth grade English teacher. She saw me struggling to become my own person and went out of her way to send me books that she thought I might or might not agree with, but would at least make me think. I remember that James Joyce's *Portrait of the Artist as a Young Man* was so infuriating. I could not understand large parts of it. Yet there I was, my own inward situation emblazoned across the pages. She once also gave me a book on Emerson. I still have that book in a special place in my library, next to the various papers, both published and unpublished, I have written on the transcendentalists over the years.

There was also that old man who picked me up by the roadside at 10 p.m., when I was hitchhiking through Wheeling, West Virginia. I was seventeen and travelling across the United States to get to college. I was idealistic, green, and naive enough to believe that, if my parents could not help me, I would do it myself. So, I got out on the road dressed in sneakers, wheatjeans, a button-down oxford shirt with a tie, madras jacket, and a cowboy hat I had borrowed from a Jewish boy scout. I also had a duffel bag full of boyhood junk, a large fire-engine-red conga drum, and a big sign that said "Dallas, Texas, by way of St. Louis or Bust." Actually, it only took me three-and-a-half days to get to my final destination, but the first night I found myself stuck outside Wheeling—no money, no food, tired. It was getting late, and I had no plans on where to sleep.

Finally, after what seemed like hours, two elderly gentlemen who were neighbors picked me up. I told them I was just trying to get across the border to Ohio that night before deciding what I was going to do. They became curious as to who I was and what I was trying to do. They stopped by a cafe and fed me dinner, and then one of them offered me a place to sleep in his guest room for the night. We talked until late. The old man seemed especially grateful to have someone in the house because his wife of fifty years had just died. We talked about philosophy and ideas and just told stories. The next morning we met for breakfast, and the two friends drove me across the bridge to the Ohio state line. My impression was that here were two holy men, although they had not meant to be that. They were beings who appeared out of the night in my hour of need. The gift we exchanged, however, was intangible, human, and personal. It was just spending a short period of time together that we knew would never be repeated, living for that brief moment. I was very young; they were very old. I was at the beginning; they were at the end of our material journey. That was all there was.

For Swedenborg, angels are inhabitants of the celestial and spiritual realms. They are predicated on the fact that human beings have two memories: an inner and an outer, or a natural and a spiritual memory. The person who lives in the merely natural world, clothed in the ego and perpetually feeding the senses, does not know that he or she has an inner memory. But the inner memory is the more vast of the two, because the things contained in the outer memory are viewed in the light of the world, while what is contained in the inner memory is in the light of heaven. While we are not usually aware of it, it is from the inner memory that we are able to speak intellectually and rationally. All we have seen or heard or spoken or done is inscribed in the inner memory, because this interior memory is, in fact, the book of our life. In the inner memory are the truths of faith and the goods of love, to employ Swedenborg's terminology. All those things that we have acquired over a lifetime from habit (and are, therefore, obscured from the outer memory) are to be found in the inner memory. Spirits and angels speak to us from the inner memory and hence have a universal language; meanwhile the languages of the world are of the outer memory, and must be learned individually until such time as we have mastered them sufficiently to interpret their universal inner meaning.

Swedenborg says that the angels are our interlocutors just after death, the ones who first talk to us of heaven, of what is good and true, and of the angelic life. But if we despised and hated these traits in physical life, in our death the angels will see into our interiors, and they will thus let us pass on, permit us to go on to the domains of our respective destinies that conform to the way we have lived and believed. God draws every spirit to himself, by means of angels and by influx, but the evil spirits within us resist and draw us down into the hells, according to Swedenborg's views.

Fechner and the
ℰ Doctrine of the Earth-Soul Ⅎ

Gustav Fechner was a German physicist and mathematician from the mid-nineteenth century who is revered by experimental psychologists as the founder of modern psychophysics. This field is the measurement of sensory thresholds and just-noticeable differences between two stimuli. It involves the physiology of the senses, the ability to recognize patterning, and so on—all the subjects fit only for a legitimate laboratory science, it is said. Historical scholarship has revealed, however, that Fechner's followers, especially in the United States, misinterpreted his agenda. Far from separating science from the spirit, Fechner believed instead that his work affirmed the reality of higher consciousness. His followers, however, contended that the mathematical formulas he bequeathed to them measure only sensations perceived from the outer world, while Fechner himself maintained that threshold differences, or between just being able to hear a sound and not hearing it, were really statements about different states of consciousness.

Fechner's view of reality was wide and far-reaching, while that of his disciples, much more narrow. To his disciples, one of his most outrageous ideas—obviously the product of a mental breakdown he once experienced, they said—was his doctrine that the Earth-Soul was man's guardian angel.[3] Fechner believed that the human race was evolving through a succession of states of consciousness, a fact that was suggested by our physiology. In the womb, we live in an aqueous environment. Yet this is the very domain in which the physical body develops from the fertilized ovum to the multicelled human being. The physical body is not primarily adapted for that state of womb consciousness. It is instead preparation for the state to come immediately after birth—normal waking consciousness in the physical environment of space.

In the same way, Fechner believed that waking consciousness in the physical body—that state in which we find ourselves now—is preparation for an even higher state of consciousness in the afterdeath plane. While we are immersed in the physical aspects of existence, we are preparing the tools we will need for the next plane, the exploration and refinement of different interior states of awareness. Rather than think of death as annihilation—the so-called nighttime view of reality in which all goes dark at the minute of death—Fechner proposed a daylight view: we are evolving to yet higher states beyond the one confined by our merely physical existence. Only some of us realize this, which completely changes the way we do things. Some know this for certain. It is an eternal verity for them. For others, there is that constant gnawing suspicion that we are, as Jorge Luis Borges once put it, "ciphers and symbols in a divine cryptography whose true meaning we do not know."[4] For the vast majority, however, such ideas make no sense. For them there is only the struggle in this life and after that, nothing. Far from dead, the universe in all its spans and wavelengths, Fechner said, is everywhere alive and conscious.

In the context of his theory, Fechner proposed that one of the things we do not readily recognize in the waking state is the true function of the earth. It is, he said, the guardian angel of all humanity. We tend to think of angels as cherubs with wings or biblical figures in human form; as a result, we have missed the larger picture. Meanwhile, the earth has all the characteristics we seek, but in a not-so-readily recognized form. The rivers are the earth's veins; the winds, its circulatory system; the seasons, its changing mood; living things, its intelligence. The earth is our vehicle through the universe. In physical form, we come from it; in life, it nourishes us; and to its body, we return.

For these reasons, we should treasure the earth, protect it, nurture it. But in our ignorance of the larger picture, which we see in Fechner's point of view, instead we mine it, gouge it, burn it, pull up its trees, dump toxic chemicals into its rivers, bury radioactive waste in its deepest caverns, and generally regard it as something to conquer. One can only wonder about the consequences of such a view.

Coincidentally, historians of psychology, rooting through the Fechner archives, found his notebooks on the doctrine of the Earth-Soul. It should come as no surprise what they discovered. One of the main sources for Fechner's inspirations was Swedenborg's writings on angels.

The Highest State
of Consciousness

Once we have it fixed in our minds that, in the process of self-realization, which is also a search for self-integration, people speak to different aspects of themselves almost as if each aspect were a different personality, and that this dialogue proceeds along definite lines of inquiry that promote intuitive insight, inspirational conclusions, and a form of healing that is the source of recovery, then we will begin to understand what is meant by a dynamic psychology of inner experience. William James best suggested the direction of this inquiry in his Gifford Lectures on Natural Religion at the University of Edinburgh, subsequently published as *The Varieties of Religious Experience*.[1]

James maintained that the central focus of religious experience is to be found not in the history of the denominational churches, the lineage of the priesthood, or a succession of texts, but rather within the interior life of the individual. He was not trying to dismiss the history of the ecclesiastical church or discount the important differences between religious traditions. He was only saying that, if we are to understand religious experience from the standpoint of psychology, then the experience of the individual has to remain primary. Theologians and devotees might concern themselves with the teachings of specific traditions; but, as James intended to address his subject from the standpoint of psychology, he told his audience that he intended to focus not on books and ideas but on the lives of individuals, on their accounts of what happened to them—in other words, his basic data would be living human documents.

James further maintained that, within the context of human experience, active exploration of the subconscious was the doorway to the awakening of ultimately transforming mystical states. By this he meant that attention turned inward toward one's own inner processes and states of consciousness presented the individual with a portal through which one could embark upon a journey of inner exploration and self-discovery. One then encountered a variety of different aspects of one's own personality.

Further, while information about various states of consciousness becomes a new focus of interest and while numerous states might be witnessed or directly experienced, it is generally agreed, and James also emphasized, that the nature of the highest states of consciousness is mystical. Such states, James said, have a noetic quality, in that they carry a sense of knowledge that plunges deeper and penetrates more widely into the farther reaches of consciousness than any other we have ever experienced. Mystical experiences tend to be ineffable, in that they far transcend any language we may wish to employ to describe them, although to try to do so, the psychologist Abraham Maslow once said, is what makes poets out of all of us. Mystical experiences are transient, in that they last for only a few moments or a few hours, although their effects may last a lifetime. We must also receive them passively. When they come on, we believe we are grasped by a superior power and must yield to the experience to get it fully. And while voluntary operations might be practiced, such as various forms of spiritual discipline, James was clear that such operations help only to set the conditions for the occurrence of these higher states; voluntary practices do not causally or automatically bring them on.

Finally, James maintained that the truths of these ultimately transforming experiences can be tested in terms of their practical results in our daily lives. By this he meant that inner experiences, to be real in the sense that rational consciousness demands, must always have some practical outcome in terms of helping us to live. According to James's pragmatic philosophy, beliefs are tested by their consequences. What one holds to be true and how one behaves are directly correlated. A psychology of inner experience that acknowledges the transforming effects of mystical states of consciousness, in other words, must always prove itself by its effect on improving the moral and aesthetic quality of everyday waking consciousness.

These are some of the primary characteristics that go into a psychology of inner experience. They presume a very simple but important model of consciousness. Adapting again from Jamesian psychology, consciousness is a field with a focus and a margin. We spend most of the time focusing on what is at the center of attention, which is usually filled up with the sights, sounds, tastes, and smells of material reality. While our attention is almost wholly directed here most of the time, what is on the margin actually controls meaning. Thoughts and objects are at the center, but feelings and intuitions—which hold the thoughts together, give them warmth, and allow them to be claimed as our own—are at the margin. These marginal perceptions lead us into the experience of subconscious states, and these interior states are the doorway, the primary route, by which the highest transforming experiences come to conscious awareness.

James's observations elucidated the nature of the highest states that human beings have reported. Because they were based on experiential first-person accounts, they carried his point directly home to the reader. But they were also largely just a piece of the picture, in the sense of depicting some prescient moment in the evolution of a particular personality. What James failed to convey was the developmental succession of such experiences over the life span in individuals who had committed their entire lives to spiritual development.

Here, for instance, is the example of Elizabeth B., a 50-year-old artist, writer, yoga teacher, and musician, who has been a practitioner of yoga for twenty-two years and involved in intensive meditation for thirteen years. She was raised in an upper-middle-class family as a Presbyterian and was graduated from Vassar College. During the 1960s, she adopted the unconventional lifestyle of a traveling musician. At that time, she went through a series of initiation experiences and now describes herself as a disciple of Paramahansa Yogananda and a member of the Self-Realization Fellowship as far as her spiritual lineage is concerned, but recounts that her practice of postures comes primarily from what she calls the Vini yoga tradition of Krishnamacharya. Over time she has experienced such heightened states as those described by James on many occasions. Her contemporary experiences are a further refinement of those she had previously experienced, as if once having them makes her prone to have them again and again.

Elizabeth is a particularly charismatic person. Many people, especially other women, are drawn to her for yoga training and advice on personal matters. As a continual seeker herself, she had struggled over a period of two years with specific problems in her daily practice. She wished to overcome old petty fears and anxieties, as well as transient reactions such as jealousy. In this present phase of her journey, she was able to find complete peace only during meditation. Then she reached a point where dramatic changes began to happen all at once:

> It all began on December 20. There had been an all day meditation . . . on the Saturday before. . . . It was lovely and the time went very quickly. The reader at the meditation asked in the words of Yogananda that Christ, in his living body, make himself known. That seemed to me an amazing thing to ask. I remember the sudden feeling of some need to respond to this and the following—that Christ consciousness is very strong this time of year. It felt as if it enveloped the earth at this time and all of us could partake of it.
>
> Then, on December 20, I got up at 5:30 a.m., went through my usual routine— recharging exercises [as given by Yogananda], *pranayams* [breathing exercises], headstand. I suddenly wanted to take a hot bath, something I never do, as it seems a bit wasteful of time. I also did *neti*—washing out the sinuses with salt water, followed by the headstand. At that time,

during the headstand, I felt a surge of peace. Peace, yes, but also this very aliveness.

After *kriyas* [chanting], I settled into listening for the AUM sound and, lo and behold! it came. At first I didn't quite accept it, thinking it was something happening outside. Then, this huge breath as if I was relaxing into a deep sleep. . . . Something seemed to lift me up in my lower back, waves of watery lights—how to describe this? And then as if light were coming from above into my head. Lifted, not having any muscles or power of my own. I kept my eyes and awareness attuned to the third eye, continuing to hear the soft but deep sound within. "Mother" came to me—the words. "Thou" came, a sense of such gratitude for all that has been given to me, even though my eyes had been veiled and I often didn't see it. Now it became clear; everything was just right, perfectly timed blissful surges of this uplifting, not within my control—although I could stop it at any time—happening to me, so beautiful, so happy. Such love. Not an emotion, but rather a state of being upheld and pierced through with love.[2]

After this episode, Elizabeth felt she had become more steady and firm. A change had come over her that she believed was enduring:

Since then, every morning the same wonderful sense of love, the same sense of being uplifted, of my eyes being pulled . . . at the Christ consciousness center. Always the words coming—Aum God, Aum Christ, Aum Yogananda, Aum

Divine Mother. I also find myself praying hard and feeling much devotion towards this Beloved Spirit, for this is what it feels like, that is what comes to mind. At times, all sound, everything fades away, and what remains is just this vast stillness. For the past six years, this Spirit-Energy has awakened me around 3 or 4 a.m., and I have experienced this wonderful feeling for several hours. I was guided to go within and allow my resisted feelings—anger, blame, jealously, and, particularly, sadness—to be, not to reject them, but to accept them and trust them. They are the doorway through which I have felt greater freedom. Spirit seems to be a "roto-rooter" par excellence: the way is down and in, not up and out.

The second example is that of a twenty-one-year-old male, working his way through college, struggling to make ends meets, yet who at the same time had embarked on a personal journey of inward exploration that had involved making certain material sacrifices in order to find the means to travel to certain spiritual places for meditation and renewal. This particular incident occurred at the top of Mount Tamalpais, north of San Francisco, at midnight:

It was an absolutely clear night on the mountain, with stars shining around a partial moon. The weather was very mild, but still cool enough for a light jacket. You could see for ten or fifteen miles in all directions. The city across the bay was lit up in great splendor and one could feel the great expanse of space from both the bay on one side of the great vista and the Pacific Ocean on the other.

My friends wandered off somewhere and I was left alone for a moment, so I decided to take the twenty-minute walk around the mountain, which was a macadam path for tourists with occasional look-out spots. I remember as I walked, deeply absorbed in my thoughts, that I began to hear the ringing in my ears, which I have used many times as a vehicle to deepen my meditation. I did not think much more about it for the moment, as my attention was suddenly pulled back to material reality by the sight of a young man wearing a headband and a sarape who was walking next to me but on the far side of the path.

We were vaguely aware of each other's presence, as he appeared to be just trying to pass me because I was walking more slowly, when all of a sudden the ringing in my ears became very loud and I was not able to modulate it as I normally could. The next thing I knew, about a dozen bats had surrounded us and began dive bombing into our hair, meanwhile letting out this high-pitched squeal that was like an extension or continuation of the ringing in my ears. But the ring was definitely coming from them because they had completely drowned out my internal sounds.

Somewhat taken off guard, I immediately crouched down on one knee, meanwhile shouting to the stranger next to me, instructing him to listen for the ringing sound in his ears. As soon as I was able to bring the ringing sound that I myself was producing back into my consciousness, the bats suddenly flew away. I stood up and hurried forward further along the path, not hesitating to look back, although I never saw the stranger again.

A little further along, still somewhat unnerved by the encounter, I came to a large branch across the path. Under the lower branch straddling the way appeared to be a snake. I again stopped dead in my tracks and crouched down to get my breath; but when I looked again, I saw that the snake was actually an unusually twisted limb of the bush that had fallen.

Relieved, I hurried under the growth and continued on down the path until I got to the lot where our car was parked. My friends were still nowhere immediately about, so I decided to sit on a park bench and wait for them. As I sat down and began to collect myself, I happened to look up into the beautiful, clear sky for my favorite constellation, Orion. Then right next to it, in a small cluster of stars which I later found out was Pleiades, the seven sisters, I suddenly had a powerful visionary experience.

Before me, with the entire universe as a backdrop, I witnessed the face of God. It was a head with beautiful but very powerful features, gaunt but strong cheeks, white skin but slightly dark and very dramatic complexion, not-quite-shoulder-length hair, and piercing eyes that radiated energy, all-intelligent, all-loving, and all-seeing. This was the picture before my eyes; but inwardly, what I was really seeing was my entire life, all there in an instant—everything that there was to know about me, with nothing hidden.

I simultaneously felt great joy and abject terror. On the one hand, it became known to me that I was not alone, that I never had been alone, and that for the rest of my life I would not be alone; that I was loved and that I could love; and that in the midst of infinite darkness, there would always be this light to illuminate my way. On the other hand, I realized in an instant that I had not lived my life in the right way up to that moment, and that the price of witnessing this truth before me was that I had to promise that I would change, that I would become the best possible person I could, and that I would dedicate myself to the service of others' welfare and to help them see clearly what I saw, if they wished to see it. I also knew from this vision that if I did not do these things, I would die. Either I would die physically, or I would die in the sense of experiencing a living death—living on but knowing I had made myself the victim of unactualized possibilities.

I made that promise then and there and I have tried to dedicate my life to the actualization of those possibilities ever since.[3]

A third example comes from Swedenborg. Although he had been struggling with spiritual questions all his life, being both the son of a Lutheran bishop and a student of Enlightenment science, Swedenborg did not experience a crisis over the struggle to reconcile religion and science until he was fifty-seven, when he began the dream diary mentioned previously. Confronted with his own consciousness as an object of scientific study, his awareness transcended the bounds of the normal waking state, and he had visions in which God came and spoke to him:

(52) I . . . fell into a sleep, and at about . . . 2:00 in the night, there came over me a strong shuddering from head to foot, with a thundering noise as if many winds beat together; which shook me; it was indescribable and prostrated me on my face. Then, at the time I was prostrated, at that very moment I was wide awake, and saw that I was cast down.

(53) Wondered what it meant. And I spoke as if I were awake; but found nevertheless that the words were put into my mouth, "And oh! Almighty Jesus Christ, that thou, of thy so great mercy, deigneist to come to so great a sinner. Make me worthy of thy grace." I held together my hands, and prayed, and then came forth a hand, which squeezed my hands hard.

(54) Straightway thereupon, I continued my prayer, and said, "Thou hast promised to take to grace all sinners; thou canst nothing else than keep thy word." At that same moment I sat in his bosom, and saw him face to face; it was a face of holy mien, and in all it was indescribable, and he smiled so that I believe that his face had indeed been like this when he lived on earth. He spoke to me and asked if I had a clear bill of health. I answered, "Lord, thou knowest better than I." "Well do so," said he; that is, as I found it in my mind to

signify; love me in reality; or do what thou hast promised. God gave me grace thereto; I found that it was not in my power. Wakened, with shudderings.[4]

If we survey the major world religions, in each one we find an esoteric inward and mystical tradition that describes a progressive journey through various realms, culminating in some kind of higher state of consciousness—*Orison* within Christianity, *samadhi* in Hindu yoga, *nibanna* in the Hinayana school of Buddhism, *sunyata* in the Mahayana, *wu* in Chinese Taoism, *kensho* or *satori* in Zen, and so on. Textbooks in the psychology of religion are replete with first-person accounts of such experiences told by the Christian mystics, the Hindu swamis, Sufi meditators, and the Chinese and Japanese sages.

Unfortunately, certain modern psychologists, especially those who study spiritual growth, refer to all such experiences as "the same," believing that there are many different roads all leading to the same higher state of spiritual consciousness. This is a particularly Western way of thinking—that all is one—and is incompatible with the way various religious traditions conceive of the ultimate in their respective systems. Its flaw is that there is no way to separate the perceiver's personal view from the fact that there could be real differences in the nature of these experiences.

The important point to establish for the present discussion, however, is that the experience of higher consciousness is a state of healing. Mystics are, after all, most closely associated with withdrawal from the world. Their esoteric visions are believed to be beyond the comprehension of ordinary men and women. They may have a unique view on reality, one that we may even describe as privileged, but essential questions remain: what is the effect of mystical awakening on everyday functioning? How is it that healing is in some way a function of consciousness?

We might address these questions by asking what are the many ways in which the relationship between the natural world and the spiritual are described and to treat these descriptions as an analogy between sickness and health. Consider, first, several different psychological interpretations. We have already mentioned the work of Victor Frankl, the Jewish psychoanalyst who survived the Nazi concentration camps and lived to develop logotherapy, a psychospiritual approach to recovery of the soul. When Frankl said there are two ways to achieve meaning—through suffering and through the actualization of values—he was describing the difference between what we do in everyday reality and what we should do if we wish to achieve the transcendent ideal.

Abraham Maslow, one of the pioneers in humanistic psychology, proposed that we look at human beings from the standpoint of a growth-oriented theory of motivation, as contrasted to a deficiency-oriented one. A growth-oriented theory of motivation tries to appeal to the best that is in people; a deficiency-oriented one always presumes the worst. With a growth-oriented outlook, one stops the car at the stop sign because there might be something new there to discover; with a deficiency-oriented one the person is afraid he or she will get a ticket for not stopping. The difference, in other words, is between a higher and a lower state of consciousness. They occur within the same environment, but appear to be radically different from one another.

Within various religious systems, a distinction is made between consciousness of the material world and the world of higher consciousness. In Vedantic Hinduism, the analogy given is to imagine the distance between your present waking state of consciousness and a higher, purer state of consciousness; and to imagine this distance as equivalent to the distance traveled from deep sleep this morning to the state you are now in. One awakens, it is said, to the realization that the material world is an illusion, or *maya*, and the only state that exists is the higher spiritual state of pure consciousness.

From a Buddhist perspective, the situation is a little more complex. The early Buddhist school of the Hinayana tradition took escape from the world of suffering as its goal. *Nibanna*—or what English-speaking audiences know as *nirvana*—is a burning out of the flame of sense desire. The two worlds, the world of suffering and the world of enlightenment, are seen as radically different. Thus, this early tradition developed into a monastic form of religion, where the monks were cloistered from the world, seeking their own personal salvation, while the society around them crumbled for lack of spiritual sustenance.

As a result, the later school of Indian Buddhism, the Mahayana, evolved a completely new goal—enlightenment sought not for the individual's own salvation, but for the sake of all others. This also necessitated a radical reinterpretation of the nature of the highest state of consciousness, which, instead of *nibanna*, became emptiness, *sunyata*. To say that all things were empty was to address directly this problem of the relationship between the world of suffering and the world of enlightenment. To the Mahayana Buddhists, both worlds are the same, meaning that one did not escape from one into the other, but rather the meditator was liberated from being enmeshed in the opposites. One was liberated while still in the body, and enlightened but still able to operate for the good of all beings who could now be helped in the midst of their own suffering. The transformation that took place in the Buddhist tradition was dramatic and produced a lineage of teachings that subsequently had a profound effect on the spread of Buddhism to Tibet, China, Korea, and Japan.

Similarly, in the opening lines of the Chinese *Tao Te Ching*, the text enjoins the seeker who wants to see the *tao* at work.[5] If one wants to see *tao* in the visible world, then one feeds the senses. If one wants to see it in the invisible world, then one stops feeding the senses. Either way, there is no value judgment implied. It all depends on which way the seeker prefers to see the *tao*. The issue of the relationship between spiritual consciousness and the material world is also expressed as *tongu zen shu* in Zen—sudden realization but gradual achievement. This means that, while the nature of reality might be seen in an instant, it takes a lifetime of gradual steps to actualize that realization. What is seen appears in a state referred to as "neither-here-nor-there," meaning not the experience of the highest state of consciousness, but rather, that moment of "just coming to," when the person is just emerging from such an experience but is still neither here nor there. In that way, both worlds are encompassed.[6]

The question of what these descriptions mean raises the additional issue of how we here in material reality can talk about states of consciousness beyond the one in which we now find ourselves. It is all very fine to delineate numerous levels or dimensions in relation to the highest state; but, in the end, these are only rational categories that may have no application in those dimensions that lay beyond the bounds of the analyzing ego, since not only the object perceived, but also the very organ of perception—consciousness—changes.

Another question concerns spiritual evolution over the life span. Most descriptions of ultimate states try to capture what is experienced in a given moment, so that we have constructed a snapshot collection of different states across different traditions. The course of interior development over the life span, however, gives us a much wider picture of a person's spiritual destiny.

In Swedenborg's case, the Swedish seer used techniques of breath control and intense concentration throughout his early life, which helped him grasp entire fields of knowledge, so he was familiar with the experience of altered states of consciousness. His dream journal shows that he went in and out of trance experiences daily before he experienced what he called an opening of the internal spiritual sense in 1744, when he believed that God first spoke to him through the angels. Subsequent spiritual openings followed, which were of varying intensities. His task was to take up a pen and God would dictate to him the true internal spiritual meaning of the books of the Bible.

This work continued for thirteen years, until 1757, when Swedenborg recounted yet another vision, but this time one of far greater significance than those that had come before. He called it the Last Judgment.[7] In this vision, Swedenborg believed that he witnessed a falling away of the denominations and the transformation of world Christianity into a collectively higher level of consciousness. The content of the vision was a picture of the Holy City described in Revelations, in which it is foretold that what is to come will be "a new heaven and a new earth." As a result of this vision, Swedenborg discontinued his former task of reinterpreting the books of the Bible and took up the composition of almost a dozen volumes describing the nature of this new dispensation. At the same time, he continued with his daily affairs as a Swedish nobleman, member of Parliament, and advisor on numerous topics ranging from mining to currency. In all other respects, his outward life appeared normal and uneventful, while his inner life continued to flourish in the knowledge that, with regard to inward states of consciousness, we live in innumerable interior worlds and that the product of personal practice will be the realization of higher states of consciousness.

These considerations suggest that spiritual healing means coming into the presence of these higher states. Sometimes we are led there providentially. Those whom we identify as healers may lead us there and invite us to be healed. Adepts systematically practice techniques to get there by altering the conditions for the occurrence of this state. Swedenborg maintained that he could enter a higher state of consciousness at will. Jesus used the revelation of Christ consciousness as a means of healing not only physical infirmity, but spiritual doubt.

But having once experienced it, what, then, is the nature of the liberated personality? What are the parallels to those personalities whom we call healers? And what are the higher laws that guide them?

Spiritual
Laws

In the spiritual sense, disease and illness come upon us when we cut ourselves off from the healing powers of the universe. This is like saying that disease invades our body all the time; we remain well only because we are strong—our immune system overcomes all invasions. We clean and otherwise maintain the temple that is our body, since it is the vehicle for the experience of higher states of consciousness; we cultivate the healing and restorative powers of sleep; and we maintain loving relationships, since love is the very life of man. In short, we have an intuitive sense for what is right and for what we should be doing.

In this sense, the spiritual laws are all within us, already carved in stone in universal and collective memory; all we have to do is look within to find them, read there the Great Book of Spiritual Instruction in which they are written, and follow their simple recipes for survival and meaning.

Injurious habits, wrong thoughts, immoral deeds, on the other hand, are our obstacles, both to health and to spiritual progress. They cut us off from the natural healing powers that are our birthright. They thwart our recovery from illness. They prevent us from living in balance with constantly changing forces around us. Anabolism and catabolism—growth and decay—are constant. The old is constantly being replaced by the new. In the beginning, anabolism is the key. From the moment of conception, there is growth everywhere; creation is the exception rather than the rule, in the sense that there is always more building than there is tearing down. Toward the end, however, catabolism gets the upper hand. We have to run twice as far to keep in shape, take the stairs twice as slowly, as well as compensate for deteriorating eyesight and an abbreviated attention span. To top it all off, we become more opinionated. In all of this we hardly need more obstacles in the form of illness and infirmity, but they creep in as extra burdens nonetheless.

Such statements remain only twists of language for some, but for others they become spiritual laws when cast into the declarative voice. They become spiritual laws for the individual when they express, as Paul Tillich once said, what is of ultimate concern to the person. There are many of them. There are different ones for different cultures and different historical periods. Each religious tradition boasts a system of them; each individual who has embarked on the inward journey towards self-realization has codified a similar list of such maxims that are true for that person and that person only. We always recognize them as spiritual laws, no matter how idiosyncratic, because when we start reciting them, everyone else starts thinking about his or her own.

At one point in my life, I taught classes in psychology and personal development to hundreds of students. They all got to hear my little maxims. In fact, they heard them so many times that, after a while, all I had to do was look as if I were going to say one of them and a hundred voices would all chime in at once, teasing me with such phrases as "every self-imposed limitation is a vehicle for its own transcendence."

Spiritual laws always tell us something about the legal system in a culture because there are always two kinds of laws—the letter of the law versus the spirit of the law, from which the letter is derived. One may well wonder how, if there are so many different cultures and so many different laws, people from different cultures can possibly get along together, let alone survive in the other's foreign culture. In fact, some do and some do not.

Abraham Maslow made some interesting points on this subject when he spoke about the characteristics of the self-actualizing personality. He said, first of all, that self-actualizing personalities from different cultures tend to be more like each other across cultures than they resemble members of their own respective cultures. This suggests that there is something universal about such people not limited by time and space that connects them to each other in ways that transcend the influence of individual societies.

Maslow also said that self-actualizing personalities tend most of the time to conform to the mores and folkways of the culture in which they live. This suggests that they are supremely adaptable and not fixed in their ways, so that they can easily learn how to fit into radically different cultures. But he also further said that a small percentage of the time they rebel against prevailing norms.

While this, of course, seems somewhat dangerous, they are also willing to sacrifice themselves for the sake of higher principles, believing that truly intelligent people have a moral responsibility to resist unjust laws. Such personalities are our movers and shakers, people who are willing to stand up for what they believe in and inspire the rest of us to follow, until an immoral situation rights itself. This was the basic principle of Gandhi's program of nonviolent noncooperation or *satyagraha*, grasping for the truth; this was Benigno Aquino, assassinated in front of world cameras as he got off the plane in his native Philippines, whose sacrifice spawned a nonviolent revolution from dictatorship to democracy. Here is Joan of Arc at the stake, and here also is the Christian account of the sacrifice of Jesus, who bore the crucifixion for the remission of others' sins.

For me, the most transfixing of ideas depicting the reality of spiritual laws has always been the Sanskrit conception of *dharma*, revered jointly by Hindus and Buddhists. *Dharma* is an extraordinarily complex word susceptible to many meanings. In one context, it means any system of laws, especially religious injunctions. In another context, it means the absolute or universal law. In yet another context, it means simply righteousness—that is, to do what one knows is the right thing. *Dharma* could also mean the Ten Commandments, since these are the codified spiritual laws of Jews and Christians; the *Manu Smriti*, which are the Hindu laws governing even the smallest of social behaviors; and the *Analects* of Confucius, which are maxims of ethical conduct. In the Buddhist tradition, there are the Three Refuges and the Eightfold Path. There is also the First Turning of the Wheel, meaning the first conversation with fellow ascetics that the Buddha had immediately after his enlightenment.

Recently, I had occasion to hear the word in a remarkably modern context. It occurred in a conversation between a man and a woman who were getting a divorce. He was a musician and she was a Buddhist meditator, and she had asked for the separation. At one point, during a particularly uncomfortable exchange about some small matter pertaining to the separation, he surprised her by saying that he hoped that they could amicably work things out, and that whatever lay in front of them, all he wanted was a divorce within the *dharma*. She was the meditator, but it was he who remembered this most interesting of Buddhist ideas.

By it, he meant that righteousness should accompany all their interactions, and that motives should be dealt with according to the spiritual law that was found by looking into the heart. He meant that uncertainty was inevitable, but there was a higher standard, albeit an intuitive one, by which they could conduct their affairs. He wished only that they could remember it. This for them was the contemporary meaning of *dharma*—in other words, the resolution of the mundane opposites into a higher spiritual reality.

We are brought back again to the essential question we started with: what is the relationship between healing and these higher states of consciousness? A partial answer may be that, in the midst of our suffering and travail, we are able to remember, even in the smallest of ways, that there is a higher state of attainment.

❦ Twelve Laws of Spiritual Healing ❧

Here, for instance, is a sample of maxims that at first I was going to call "The Twelve Laws of Spiritual Healing"; but, in deference to my old friend, the late Henry

A. Murray, I will just refer to them as "twelve" laws of spiritual healing, to let everyone know that any number might be possible. The principle in every one of them is the same, however; healing always involves the experience of higher consciousness.

Love is the only answer. The first law has for its basis forgiveness. One of the key psychological sources of illness is anger, which means that we are carrying around a great deal of submerged hatred. Usually, this anger is directed toward some person of our immediate acquaintance, but it could also be attached to something more abstract, like a group of people or a particular institution. In the end, we have to ask ourselves what it is that really matters. The amount of money we have accumulated? The number of cars we have in the driveway? How famous we have finally become? No, I would say that, in our hour of greatest need, or in our hour of greatest need of another, the answer is that nothing really matters but how we have loved.

Swedenborg himself said that love is the key because cultivation of the right emotions allows the intellect to comprehend what is spiritual. Love is feeling—an intuitional emotion. Love transcends ideas. Love is eternal, even if the feelings change later, because once you have loved and have been loved in return, its effects are permanent. Love is forgiveness, because it is larger than momentary episodes of disappointment. Love more than conquers all; as Swedenborg said, "Love is the life of man."[1]

We are never alone in the universe. Illness tends to isolate us from the flow of contemporary events. We have less energy, infirmities might prevent more extensive movement; we may be contagious, or just worried about our appearance. Depression is a common but often unrecognized accompaniment of physical illness.

All of these circumstances might make us feel that we have been abandoned and that we are alone.

Far from it. In the spiritual sense, all who have ever loved us are right there; and all whom we are related to by blood who have passed from the scene stand before us in the invisible world. Then, within the Christian scheme, there is always the relationship we have to our Maker. There is the well-known story of a man after death talking to Jesus. He was complaining that the road of life had been so hard, and Jesus seemed to walk with him only periodically. At the hardest times, when he looked back, he only saw a single set of footprints in the sand, believing he had to walk those moments alone. "Not so," replied Jesus. "Didn't you know that at those moments it was I who was carrying you?"

We should cultivate the higher emotions. This is a very Buddhist idea but also a Swedenborgian one. Normally, when we are enmeshed in the material world, our emotions are governed by pleasurable and painful attachments to objects of sense desire. We experience pain even at the height of pleasure, because we often desecrate the moment with the thought that the pleasure will not last. At the same time, we invest permanency in material reality and are always destined to be disappointed when things change or when we finally realize that we have had our priorities in the wrong order, because, in reality, the natural is a mere product of the spiritual, not the other way around.

One antidote for this, the Buddhists have said, is to cultivate the higher emotions. Instead of always being the victim of circumstance, tossed around by the vagaries of emotion, we should cultivate the will, which the Swedenborgians say is the means by which we govern the affections. Self-love, for instance, can be transmuted into love for others, reverence for life, or compassion for all living beings down to the last blade of grass, or into the love of God. An even-temperedness cultivated toward acquisition and loss in the material world can be elevated to equanimity toward all things. Passional emotions tie us to the earth, while spiritual ones free us to course in higher wisdom, say the Buddhists.

Spontaneity is an important key to recovery. Spiritual power comes to us, according to Swedenborg, when we open ourselves to an influx of divine energy. By this, he meant surrender to the higher will, to the higher power. To do this, we must release tension, let go of certainty, sometimes even forego reason, and instead invest all we have in faith, believing that what is good will come to us. So opened, we are then more susceptible to the workings of Divine Providence. Just as paradox is a primary characteristic of life's most extraordinary moments, so too are chance meetings, fortuitous turns of events, mistakes that turn out to be unexpected gifts. Jung called it synchronicity; James called it tychism. The new name for it in science is chaos theory, where the rationalists believe they see consistent but nonlinear patterns in disorder.

To be led by Divine Providence is to give oneself up completely to the life of the spirit—not to know the outcome or perhaps even the path, but to trust in forces larger than oneself that everything will come out right in the end. At the height of our illness, we hardly feel creative. In the face of our infirmity, we shrink from the unknown, seeking to adjust or adapt to the new limitations of our circumstance. But not all people are like that. Some take infirmity as a gift and are led to new and liberating attitudes; others may rise above their circumstances through innovative adjustments that have new and unexpected outcomes in relationships and work as well as belief.

We should always remain loyal to something. This was the injunction of the American Protestant philosopher Josiah Royce, in speaking about the patient's task, even for those who were confined in bed.[2] Always commit yourself to something, have a goal to strive for, allow yourself to be gripped by a great idea or a noble cause. Try to end world hunger, achieve world peace, attain freedom for prisoners of conscience. Work to save the whales, end poverty, organize support groups for terminal cancer patients, become an advocate for daycare for all working mothers. Whatever the theme, make the commitment to something more than you have ever done. Make it something that will inspire you to rise above your present circumstance, keep in constant contact with people, watch over those who are less fortunate, or make those who are more powerful more accountable. Imagine transforming the world even from one's death bed, never giving up until the end. Never stop fighting for life; never give up hope; never waiver in your cause until you have achieved your goal.

Illness can be creative. Often we think of sickness as something transitory; but, for millions of people, illness is chronic, even lifelong. The loss of limbs, a radical disfigurement, terrible pain, all of these may be permanent adjustments that a person has to make. Chronic illness, however, can also be a stimulus to kinds of internal growth that would not have been otherwise possible. The last sixteen years of Freud's life, during which time he radically reformulated psychoanalysis, was dominated by his struggle with nasal cancer. Beethoven composed symphonies while completely deaf. Jackson Pollock, as well as numerous other artists, used conditions of psychopathology to produce new dimensions in modern art. Indeed, genius and insanity were allied together in the nineteenth century, and psychologists still persist in thinking that a little madness ferments in the dough of which great men and women are made.

The link is not sacrosanct, however. As F. W. H. Myers once put it, the only reason we confuse creativity with insanity is that both dimensions of inner experience come to waking consciousness through the same channels, so rationality always confuses them as the same.[3] The psychological point is that, while terrible things might happen to us, there is simply no telling what new doors will open up for us in our response to pain, sickness, and infirmity. Our illness can always become the vehicle toward the actualization of a spiritual destiny higher than the physical or psychological.

Pain is friendly. According to this truism, pain is not always the enemy. While we would think that everyone's natural reaction is to shirk from any kind of painful experience, pain might also be a stimulus to wake us up to a higher reality, where we can more amenably manage that which would normally be intractable. As is well known, one of the primary characteristics of altered or dissociated states of consciousness is the phenomenon of anesthesia. We may enter such states spontaneously. Remember the case of the returning Korean war veteran cited previously. As a prisoner of war, he remembered waking in the middle of the night in his cell because he had heard someone scream down the hall in pain. The next moment, however, he realized that it was, in fact, he who was screaming and he who was being tortured.

On the other hand, pain may also be a teacher to help us learn techniques in the voluntary control of internal states. The well-know physician and hypotherapist Milton Erikson, for instance, struggled with polio as a young man, which later led him to study hypnosis as a self-medicating strategy. Today, his pioneering techniques lead the field of clinical hypnotherapy.[4]

There are also instances where pain tells us that we are still alive. Athletes who train vigorously know this; they are not so much numb to pain as they are adapted to higher and higher levels of it. Similarly, in the midst of severe trauma, constant pain is often replaced by numbness. One of the marks of psychological recovery is the ability to call forth the pain so that we gain some control over it, rather than have it fester in the unconscious, controlling thoughts and behavior according to its own laws.

Winning may really mean winning over the mind of discord within oneself. On this point, we should always be aware that the source of our greatest suffering might not be so much some external force— the other person, the relative we have always hated, the stranger who has offended us, the institution that appears uncaring in our moment of greatest need, the metal wheelchair to which we are confined. The problem may be based in conflicts within ourselves about which we are not fully aware. These we tend to project out onto the world and clothe in the garb of some other person, group, or object. Regardless of what happens externally, our own peace of mind is what counts. The way to win with the insurance companies is not blindly to battle them head on, but to resolve conflicts within ourselves that dramatically change the conditions of the outward encounter, which may allow the exchange to come to a completely different and unexpected end.

Battling illness can mean much the same thing. Inner conflict weakens the immune system, puts us at greater risk for infection, and diverts our attention from the real task at hand—self-healing. The biggest obstacle to our own progress in any sphere may be our entrenched prejudices, intense feelings we have never resolved, or ambivalence we have stored away over the years about highly charged emotional subjects. This leads us to a corollary of the above rule.

Sickness can be a message about unfinished business. Sometimes we can get ourselves in a situation where we are overwhelmed by events in life. This is often made worse when successive experiences befall us all at the same time. Here is a man who got divorced, lost his job, and then had his children taken away. Here is a woman whose beloved father has died, the state has taken her house to make room for a new roadway, and her company has just been bought out by a bigger business that plans to eliminate her job. Is it any wonder that such individuals would retreat into illness?

There is also the circumstance where situations build up because we ignore them until they get so big that we believe they can no longer be dealt with. A minor wound left untreated could lead to gangrene if it got infected. Filthy living conditions are the ideal breeding ground for infectious diseases. Smoking cigarettes may be alternatively a pleasure and an annoyance until the first signs of cancer, when we might believe that quitting may be too late. Similarly, psychological conflict can have the same effect—the alcoholic parents who are estranged from their child—just a phone call away until he committed suicide; the widow who has just lost her loving companion of a lifetime who herself pines away until death. In these cases, sickness can be a message that we have unfinished business to attend to. Clean that wound; scour that room; call that child; rise up and make new friends. Always, on the road to recovery and health, we may be called upon to deal with what we have put off as too insignificant because we believe we are plagued with bigger problems. The antidote may just be to start small, take a first step, and move one day at a time.

Thought is a vehicle for its own transcendence.
This law encourages us to let consciousness get beyond
labels, get beyond words, even get beyond the stream of
everyday cognitive thoughts. Illness often brings with it
incessant brooding. It can bring obsessive attempts to ra-
tionalize why we have become ill. It can inhibit the production of insight and can close the door to the entrance
of noncognitive experiences that may be essential to our
recovery.

There are thoughts, for instance, that take us to the
very edge of conceptualization rather than deeper into
analytic ideas. Under this rubric, we find the injunction
to remember religious ideas, to cultivate high thoughts,
and to accept that, while words have the power to both
hurt and heal, silence can also be a great lawgiver as far
as spiritual understanding is concerned. Here also poetry
is food for the soul and nourishment for the spirit in
ways that narrative words or logical reasoning can never
be.

Also, certain kinds of spiritual teachings can liberate us the instant we hear them. In Hindu yoga, such
spiritual teachings are meant to have two purposes: to
burn out the seeds of past thoughts that keep us bound
in the cycle of rebirth and to articulate spiritual ideas
that themselves leave no karmic traces. The Buddhist
idea of emptiness, for instance, is meant to liberate the
mind from attachment to opposing arguments about the
nature of ultimate reality. Since emptiness is also
thought to be empty of itself, the philosopher does not
cleave to that idea either. Historically, the emptiness
doctrine is the forerunner to the Zen *koan*, the nonra-
tional riddle given to the student by the teacher in order
to free the mind from attachment to rational thought:
"When you die and they scatter your ashes to the wind,
where are you?" "Even though the mind is like a mirror,

if Zen is the realization of no-mind, then what is there to polish?" "Where does the white go when the snow melts?" and so on.

The difference between life and death may not be gradual. Here we are enjoined that the common perception that life slips away gradually leading to death might be an illusion. In the same way that Buddhism and Christianity, or Taoism and Islam cannot be blithely compared without getting into the details of the different systems of thought, life and death may not be just two opposite ideas. In both cases, we may be talking about different epistemological frames of reference, totally different states of consciousness, radically different worlds that may, in the end, not be comparable. Illness and death are, after all, ideas conferred upon experience in the waking rational state. Who is to say that they are not actually something else when that state actually obtains? We all know of circumstances where people who are not really that sick give up the will to live and die in spite of anything we do. Or there are people whose illness or injury is so severe that there is no chance they will survive, yet who seem to recover completely against all reason. Similarly, we have a glut of examples of people apparently dying and then coming back to life to report what they saw in the next realm. We can never be sure, however, how far they actually got, since we do not really know where they went. All we have is their cognitive perceptions upon returning, which are comprehensible only in our present collective state of consciousness.

Swedenborg spoke to these epistemological leaps when he talked about the difference between the natural, the spiritual, and celestial worlds—the world of man, the world of angels, and the world of God. The differences between them, he said, are not continuous; they are discrete. There is no gradual step-by-step progression from one plane to the next; there is only penetration into a deeper and wider reality that leaves everything about the old state completely behind. You cannot get there from here, in other words. Heaven is not a physical place; it is a state of consciousness. To get to heaven, one does not simply walk or drive; one needs to experience a complete transformation of consciousness. And in this sense, it has also been said that spiritual disciplines provide us with a simulation of the death experience while still alive in the body. Whether or not this really prepares us, however, is a mystery still to be answered.

It is permissible to die alone. This law is actually more of a suggestion. Some people want to be alone to recover. Their illness is too personal. They have always borne their suffering most successfully by themselves. It may be similar with the hour of death. Everyone may rush in and continue to mill around. Everyone might believe that it is terrible to die alone with no one nearby. Everyone may covet the opportunity to be present at such a momentous occasion, the passing of a soul out of the body toward heaven. But it may in the end all depend on the personality and temperament of the dying. The person may wait until we step away from the bedroom to pass from the scene. Perhaps there was a long standing pact that the person has made with him- or herself; some people would rather be remembered as they were in the blush of health than in the wasted condition of death. We should consider the inmost wishes of the dying person as well as the dictates of social convention. Death, after all, may not be all bad. There may be numerous examples of a good death; of a peaceful death; of a death that may have some suffering, to be sure, but still free of physical pain. The spirit may live in the physical body according to the laws of society, but in the end it will die according to laws of its own.

Healing
Personalities

According to Swedenborg, some people believe that to live a life that leads to heaven—that is, to lead a spiritual life—is difficult because they have to renounce the world, divest themselves of the lusts of the flesh, and live apart from others. They think that they must reject worldly things such as riches and honors, that they must continuously meditate on God, contemplate salvation and eternal life, be in constant prayer, and always be thinking spiritual thoughts. This they suppose is the definition of how to live in the spirit and not in the flesh. Swedenborg had learned from experience and by conversation with angels, however, that this is not so; moreover, he learned that those who follow this ascetic path are not always free from sorrow, nor do they always experience the joy of heaven. This is because a person's life always remains with him and him alone. In order to receive the life of heaven, we need to live in the world and engage in its business and its employments, and through this moral and civil life, receive what is spiritual. In no other way can spiritual life be formed within us, or can our spirit be prepared for heaven. For to live internally while ignoring the external is to become a shut-in, a recluse, like a house without a foundation, which can only sink or fall.[1]

Translated into contemporary terms, the problem is that there seems to be a wide discrepancy between the life of the modern physician, who presents him- or herself as thoroughly enmeshed in the world, and the mystic, who has withdrawn into divine contemplation. Swedenborg's answer to this dilemma is clear. Spiritual self-actualization is the province of every person. While the individual might not have the technical expertise of the modern scientifically trained physician, and is therefore unable to treat complex physical diseases as a specialist would, every person has the capacity to heal from a spiritual standpoint.

If so, we should then ask not, "What is the personality of the healer?" but rather ask, "How do I actualize that part of my own personality that has the power to heal spiritually?" Physical medicine actually gives us a photographic negative of that standard. The spiritual healer is a generalist, while the scientific physician is a specialist. The spiritual healer believes that the natural world is derived from the spiritual, while the modern physician perhaps does or does not give any credence to a domain of experience beyond the physical, the sensory, and the rational.

Of course, while there does appear to be an overemphasis on scientific reductionism in modern medicine, and while physicians tend to occupy a privileged place in the progression of lives, they still have a human side. They see life from birth to death; they see the worst cases of disease and illness; they are the ultimate conservators of the most chronic cases, the incurables, those maimed for life, those in chronic pain. They have their scientific sensibilities, but they also have their humanity. To be sure, it is a byproduct of everything else they have been taught; it is often suppressed in order to work on a cadaver or someone mortally wounded. But as human beings, physicians, too, have their limits. There is always a point beyond which each person cannot go. I am reminded of two examples: one is a case of embarrassed compassion; the other, of accidentally programmed medical depression.

The first example was a case presentation in psychiatric grand rounds at the Massachusetts General Hospital, delivered by the distinguished psychiatrist Dr. Lawrence Kolb. The presentation was a video-cassette recording on drug-induced catharsis for post-traumatic stress disorder. The technique was to administer a drug to the patient in a hospital setting that would relax him and facilitate talking out the traumatic memories. Meanwhile, the sound of machine guns and mortar fire was played in the background to trigger the old memories. Dr. Kolb narrated to the audience while the tape was played. At one point, on hearing the machine-gun fire, a patient began to tremble uncontrollably as the therapy proceeded. As that part came up on the tape, Dr. Kolb apologized to the audience and explained that what we were about to see was not an example of the physician's over-involvement with the patient. What showed on the tape was Dr. Kolb moving to the bedside to hold the shaking man in his arms until he calmed down. It was a touching scene that easily could have been interpreted as emotional over-identification on the part of the attending physician.

What I saw, however, was the tremendous humanity of this physician, spontaneously given in a moment of desperate need to a human being in dire straits. The discussion of the episode that followed centered around what the psychiatrists called transference-counter-transference issues, meaning unresolved sexual issues projected onto the therapist by the patient (called the transference), and onto the patient by the therapist (called the counter-transference). At that moment, modern medicine and psychiatry seemed to over-emphasize the objective and the analytic; it was not unresolved sexual issues at the heart of that experience, but an instance of true human caring that spontaneously erupted into an otherwise objectively controlled scientific environment.

The other example is a different one about a scientific physician's limits. The physician was a world-class dermatologist, cited as one of the four best specialists in his field. Here was a man at the top of his profession. Yet he had been deeply wounded psychologically by a year he had spent as a combat surgeon in Vietnam. He had even written a book as a way to make sense out of his experience.

The book, however, turned out to have a truly existential ending. According to him, the soldiers in combat could not always figure out why they were there or what they were fighting for. The nationalism and the patriotic fervor of World War II could not be recreated in that place. It all seemed pointless; the United States government itself was even at war with its own people, and the government appeared to many of the soldiers to be wrong in its military involvement in Vietnam. Indecision and uncertainty were everywhere.

The doctor himself worked in a chaotic milieu. He was in a privileged position as an M.D. and an officer, to be sure. But he paid a deep price with his peace of mind for that vantage point. Life was intermittently slow and leisurely, then suddenly chaotic and full of intense suffering. Nothing would happen for hours, perhaps days; then suddenly helicopters would bring in staggering numbers of wounded. There was always a rush to get to the injured and dying. Happenstance oftentimes seemed the only law that directed the attention of the small staff amid the sea of bodies. If the doctor turned to those on the right, precious seconds were lost and those on the left would die that day. If he turned to the left, those on the right would die first.

The book slowly chronicled a dangerously deterio rating condition, especially for those who were trying to survive psychologically, even if they were not being shot at. There was a blurring of the line between life and death, until the soldiers could no longer tell the difference. Everyone who could remain sane was caught in that no-man's land in the middle; and as a result, the brightest and sharpest, the best that scientific medicine could produce, were forced to live unendingly in that altered state of paradoxical consciousness. Each episode of their daily lives was a caricature, a tableau; dark humor was only a momentary release; anomie, emotional wasting, was common. What would normally have been wisdom became jaded—liquid television, a black vision in the extreme.

In contrast to the scientific specialist who must compartmentalize to survive in his or her field, everyone has the healing dimension within normal personality. However, although everyone has it, few develop it systematically. Many manifest parts of it quite spontaneously without knowing that is what they are doing. They were just born that way; their mother or their father was like that, so they are that way as well. They become what accident and circumstance permit them to become. They are good but incomplete examples of how the power to heal from a spiritual standpoint develops.

To develop the spiritual side of personality, however, analytical and abstract thinking must give way to intuitive insight and to the domain of the imaginal. The spiritual dimension of personality lauds the devotional, the attitude of faith, the sense of the intuitive. It grows as we come to appreciate the musical, the artistic, and the poetic side of our nature. We should foster the continuously flowing stream of insights, meditative concentration, a wide knowledge of spiritual subjects across cultures, the descent of consciousness into the body, the ability to be spontaneous and to love unconditionally. We should cultivate our clairvoyant capacities and our tendencies to experience ecstatic states, for the spiritual side of personality is also the side of personality capable of spiritual healing.

I want to make two important points about this side of human personality. The first pertains to egolessness, while the second pertains to the experience of psychic phenomena.

Concerning egolessness, the primary question is, "Is such a state even possible?" Can we ever transcend the bounds of ego-consciousness? Can we ever really get out of the body while we are in it? Can we ever act as if we had no personal identity? Can we ever get into a state where material reality slips away, where there is no time, or at least where there is a different sense of time? I answer, "Yes!" And, to the people who say, "No!" I say they have never experienced an opening of the internal spiritual sense; they have never left the bounds of ego-consciousness or transcended material reality. If they did, they did not know what happened to them, so they retreated back to the familiar, to the normal, to the physical, and to the rational as fast as they could. Of course, they will say that such transcendence is not possible; but it is simply not within the realm of their experience, or not within their comprehension.

The sense that we have lost our personal identity is actually quite common. The concentration camp prisoner who is just a tattooed number; the divorcee whose church does not recognize her as either married or single; the excitement of completely losing our head in a frenzied crowd; the dissociation of consciousness that can accompany massive head injuries, any kind of near-death experience—these are all examples of forced egolessness. There are others that are more benign—acts of selflessness in which someone gives his or her life to save another; the voluntary act of silence in a Trappist monastery, where one might not hear one's name uttered for years; the consciousness of a newborn baby in the months and years before there is a clear sense of personal identity; the transport of ecstasy in a visionary experience; washing the feet of another—all these are potential, egoless human experiences.

On the one hand, egolessness, even if it is only a transitory state, is the means by which awareness is permitted to enter into internal domains beyond cognitive thought and discursive language. On the other hand, it is also one of the most important protective mechanisms awareness has from being blinded or otherwise bound to the energy of alternative states of consciousness far more powerful than the normal waking state can handle. The greatest danger of the inward journey is narcissistic identification of ourselves with the power that flows through us, a power greater than the individual.

In states of spiritual healing, we are mere conduits for a higher power; we are not necessarily that power. To pretend we are is to lose the camouflage of invisibility that awareness needs to navigate different dimensions of the interior domain. To pretend we are something that we are not is to fixate in that state, to be trapped, now knowing that this is not the end but merely a byway and not the main path. In this fixation, we understand that we have to live out the karma of identifying with a lower state, knowing all the while that higher states exist but we cannot get to them. Perhaps we are now imprisoned for an eternity. Who knows? The time sense is so different. Egolessness, then, is both our vehicle and our shield.

The second point I want to make concerns the alleged development of psychic powers. All the esoteric traditions describe such powers, while Western science denies them completely. For this reason, they hold an unusual place in modern American culture—the subject of pulp magazines, daytime television talk shows, and 900 numbers. Notwithstanding the myopia of our own culture, there is a several-thousand-year-old tradition of non-Western ideas that takes the reality of psychic phenomena quite seriously.

My own opinion from a study of these older traditions is that psychic phenomena readily occur in many individuals, but more frequently in those predisposed to internal self-discovery. Moreover, these capacities are trainable, but not in the ways usually described. Their purpose, in my opinion, is not to find the perfect mate or lost wallets or missing dead bodies as we do in the West. Rather, they are an epiphenomenon in the process of self-realization. They are byproducts of self-knowledge—nothing more—and they function primary as guideposts to one's level of spiritual progress.

Psychic abilities occur spontaneously in certain people who have these capacities from birth; but usually these individuals do not know how they got these powers, and they are functionally incapable of teaching them to someone who does not already have them. According to the yoga texts, supernormal powers are trainable and can be consistently produced, but they are the result of yoga teaching, not its source or its goal. This means that healers might demonstrate these capacities and even use them on others for spiritual healing and personal development; but, in this way, such powers function much as they did when Jesus demonstrated them, namely as means to set a person on the path to righteousness.

ℰ Healers of Souls and Nations ℱ

The reader will be sorely disappointed if he or she believes that I will cite examples such as Madame Curie, or the great surgeon Harvey Cushing, or even Peter the psychic surgeon from Brazil. Rather, here I address the idea of healing personalities. Such persons may not have performed operations on sick people or dispensed medicines to the ill, but each in his or her own way heal wounded souls or showed themselves capable of binding the wounds of nations. I offer them only as examples of people who have embarked on a spiritual quest who, mostly without realizing it, by their very nature have had the capacity to inspire others to become whole.[2]

The first of these is the late Tenzing Norgay Sherpa. I met Tenzing in 1979, when I went on a trip to India and Sikkim. We were at first going to the Hunza Valley near Kashmir, but, unfortunately, it was a tense time in the region. The American ambassador had been killed in Afghanistan. The Chinese were running arms through the Hunza Valley to the Afghan resistance; and, in the valley, anyone who was Caucasian was presumed to be a Russian and shot on sight. Meanwhile, ownership of the Hunza Valley was being disputed by five different countries.

As an alternative, I was able to arrange a tour into southwestern Sikkim, a protected religious area in the northeast corner of India. The tour was led by Tenzing Norgay, the man who had taken Sir Edmund Hillary to the top of Everest for the first time in 1953, and the goal was to visit a few of the Buddhist monasteries down in the jungle and then climb to the base camp of Mount Kenchenjunga, the training area of Tenzing's Himalayan Mountaineering Institute, situated at an altitude of 18,000 feet.

The trek lasted three weeks during which time we walked seventy-five miles up into the Himalayas and back, starting in Darjeeling, India. It was the last trek of the season, just before the winter snows. There were supposed to be twenty people in our climbing party, but most had canceled out at the last minute because our plane from the United States had to fly over Iran to get to India. It was near the end of the Iranian hostage crisis, and most people, we were told, were afraid the Iranians might down our plane with a guided missile. As a result, only four showed up, but Tenzing decided to go on with the trek anyway. In addition to us four trekkers, there were Tenzing's son and grandson, five of Tenzing's top Sherpas, and twelve porters, besides Tenzing himself.

We started out in Darjeeling, went into Sikkim by truck, and began our walk at Yuksum, at 5,000 feet. As it happened, we were thwarted by bad weather and difficult climbing conditions, and just made it up to 14,000 feet, above the snow line where the glaciers begin, before we had to turn back. As a result of this early return to the lower altitude, we had extra time on our hands, which we spent down in the jungle, touring a number of out-of-the-way Buddhist monasteries that were normally closed to foreign climbing parties. Most of these temples had been abandoned since India had naturalized Sikkim, and the monks came only once a year to chant the particular texts in each attic library. At Tashiding, we found an active monastery with a head monk, Lama Dup, and a school for Tibetan refugee children.

During this period, we made fast friends with Tenzing's son and grandson who were on the trek with us; and, because I spoke a little Hindi, we also spent extra time with Tenzing and the sherpas.

Tenzing Norgay. Here was a man, already in his early seventies, with an extraordinarily tight and wiry build, who was born in Nepal and had been climbing on these glaciers all his life. Although he could neither read nor write, he spoke five languages and was a world-renowned personality. Despite his large reputation, I found him to be extraordinarily quiet and soft spoken, a man totally unselfconscious. His manners were gracious; his dress—climbing boots, English walking knickers, knee socks, a flannel shirt, and a jaunty cap—I would describe as almost natty. His son and grandson, both fifteen, adored him, and the sherpas worshipped the ground he walked on. The porters were genuinely respectful and in many ways equally awed.

In the three weeks I was with him, we had many chances to talk. I found him extraordinarily wise, not only about the mountains, but also about human nature. His intelligence was keen and refreshingly uncluttered. I also found, by talking to as many people who lived in the area as I could, that he was revered as a hero of Asia because he was the only hill sherpa known all over the world. He had brought international attention to his people and their way of life, almost all of it in some way good and beneficial. He was in every way equal to his British counterpart, and this elevated the self-respect of those who most closely identified with him. He was a fierce supporter of the Tibetans in exile who had fled the Communist Chinese invasion of their country, and he used his considerable influence to help the Tibetan cause wherever he could. Moreover, fame had not changed him; if anything, it made him even more of who he was at the beginning. I felt at great peace in his presence. I also believe that he is the closest thing to a *bodhisattva* that I have ever met.

I have also been inspired spiritually by people with excruciating disabilities who have not only compensated for them but, by their accomplishments, have continually challenged the walking well to take a second look at their own untapped human potential. One example is the life of Dr. Anthony Sutich, a licensed clinical psychologist and pioneer co-founder of humanistic and transpersonal psychology in the United States. He died in 1976 at the age of 72. As a teenager in the early 1920s, Sutich was severely injured when he was accidentally hit on the side of the head by a bat during a baseball game. His attempt at recovery was hampered by the onset of neurological degeneration, so that, within a few years, he became completely paralyzed; for the rest of his life, he was confined to a gurney. He could still speak, however; move his head from side to side; and move the hand on one arm. Meanwhile, his internal functions continued to work, while the rest of him remained completely motionless.

Undaunted, Sutich became a tireless labor organizer and social reformer. He also arranged to continue his education from the bedside. He coerced, cajoled, and inspired many people, especially others who were handicapped, and soon became a counselor even to his own tutors, who were not disabled. Through his connections in Palo Alto, California, where he lived, he was permitted to sit in on psychology courses at Stanford University, as long as he could find graduate students to carry him on the gurney up the five flights of stairs to the lecture hall. At Stanford, he met Ernest Hilgard, a professor of psychology, distinguished learning theorist, and researcher on hypnosis, who aided considerably in furthering Sutich's career.

By the 1940s Sutich had a flourishing psychotherapeutic practice, largely because his orientation was so unusual—he was most interested in personal growth and spiritual development in his clients at a time when clinical psychology had veered off into psychoanalysis and the idea that all personal problems were the result of a sexual neurosis. After Hilgard introduced him to psychologists on the national scene, such as Gordon Allport at Harvard, Sutich was grandfathered-in as a member of the American Psychological Association and licensed as a California psychologist, although he had no university degrees.

In 1949, Sutich teamed up with the motivational psychologist Abraham Maslow, and eventually the two of them launched the *Journal of Humanistic Psychology* and its attendant professional group, the American Association of Humanistic Psychology, which became influential in the development of the human potential movement in the United States. Several thousand psychologists flocked to their association, believing that humanistic psychology and the development of human potential represented the wave of the future.

As I mentioned in the introduction, I first met Anthony Sutich in 1969 through the aging personality-social psychologist Gardner Murphy. I flew out to California and had several interviews with Sutich, we corresponded, and he introduced me to the younger generation of psychologists around him, including James

Fadiman and Robert Frager. By then, Maslow and Sutich had created yet another organization and another journal around the idea of what they called transpersonal psychology, the study of meditation, spiritual disciplines, and higher states of consciousness.

I became involved in these activities; presented papers at the early transpersonal conferences; and embarked on various training regimes in yoga, meditation, and aikido as a part of my own continued work in psychology. Maslow died in 1970, and Sutich followed in 1976. Sutich received his doctorate on his deathbed, for a historical study on the founding of humanistic and transpersonal psychology. The degree was awarded by the Humanistic Psychology Institute, now an accredited Ph.D. program operating as the Saybrook Institute, which Sutich had helped to found.

Researchers, psychologists, therapists, educators, physicians, and social thinkers associated with Maslow and Sutich have since gone on to become pioneers in the voluntary control of internal states, alternative therapies, holistic health, and energy medicine—areas that are driving a major psychospiritual revolution in America today and changing the face of health care at the level of the delivery of clinical services. While he could not have foreseen that it would take exactly this form, this was the vision that Sutich fostered from his gurney and helped to bring about over almost a half century of work.

Yet another type of healing personality is Elie Wiesel. Winner of the Nobel Peace Prize, Wiesel is a survivor of the Nazi concentration camps, an interpreter of the Jewish experience throughout history, a contemporary social commentator, and a major voice of reconciliation between Jews and Arabs in the Mideast. My judgment of him is that he is just a man. Yet he has obviously seen dimensions of human experience that I can never know, and this has melded his character in ways that call forth the higher dimensions of humanity rather than the lower for anyone in his presence, regardless of how mundane the topic is that he might be addressing.

It is always easy to romanticize people and to elevate them to dimensions that they themselves could not imagine, simply through projection. But this is precisely my point. When we are in the presence of individuals who have committed themselves to the actualization of the spirit, we tend to be elevated to that dimension within ourselves. Wiesel is very quiet and soft spoken; I cannot imagine him raising his voice. It would not be necessary. One only needs to hear his voice, which communicates a spiritual force that has the power to command attention and to change others. These are the spiritual qualities of that healing dimension within personality.

I want to say a final word about the Dalai Lama, the spiritual leader of the Tibetan people and winner of the Nobel Peace Prize in 1989, whom I have met only once. The occasion was his trip to Boston to visit the Tibetan community in the fall of 1995. This community, one of almost two dozen Tibetan clusters around the United States, came about due to the efforts of Edward Bednar, a Catholic by birth and also a Buddhist meditator. With a group of other private citizens, Bednar lobbied for federal legislation that was eventually included in the 1990 Immigration Act, permitting one thousand stateless Tibetans to enter the United States and become legal citizens.

The Tibetans were driven into exile forty-five years ago when the Chinese Communists invaded their country; and while six million Tibetans now remain under genocidal conditions in occupied Tibet, virtual prisoners in their own country, the Tibetan government-in-exile continues to exist in the free world, with 118,000 followers, most of whom are guests of the people of India. There are Tibetan communities in Burma and Switzerland, as well.

The 1990 Immigration Act, among many other things, recognized Tibetans as stateless persons. That meant that the one-thousand Tibetans had entered the United States as immigrants, not refugees, so that there was no public money provided for resettlement. Accordingly, Bednar and his colleagues, in coordination with the Office of Tibet in New York City, founded the Tibet-US Resettlement Project, which raised money, found jobs, and located sponsors for all thousand Tibetans. The plan was to establish the Tibetans in twenty-one different cluster sites around the United States, both to preserve Tibetan culture and to provide an introduction to the American and democratic way of life.

The Boston cluster site, beginning with only fifty Tibetans, has since swelled to 185. On the Dalai Lama's visit, 500 Tibetans assembled, plus a large number of guests. Two years prior to his visit, I had been able to arrange for the Swedenborg Chapel at Harvard-Radcliffe to provide space for cultural activities of the Tibetan Association of Boston and also an office for the Tibet-U.S. Resettlement Project. As a result, a relationship developed between the Swedenborgians and the Tibetans, and the officers of the church and members of the senior women's alliance were invited to meet briefly with the Dalai Lama.

When I went through the reception line, I found myself quite speechless. I thought of telling the Dalai Lama a little about who I was, but this seemed extraordinarily narcissistic on my part. I could not think of a single historic or dramatic thing to say, even though four thousand years of Asian history and philosophy, the history of Buddhism in Tibet, the last forty years of the Tibetan exile, and the entire history of the Resettlement Project and the Boston cluster site suddenly flashed across my mind. So, I just said, "Thank you" a few times as I shook his hand. I noted immediately that he was completely there with me; and, despite the fact he had just shaken one hundred other hands, I had his absolute attention. He was completely calm and genuinely present and he spoke in those familiar low tones that characterize his speeches, saying now merely "Thank you" in return.[3]

Such personalities heal because within themselves they are a moving presence. They influence others in ways of which they are not aware. They appeal to the healing dimension in our own personality and, in this way, are responsible for a wide-ranging spiritual wave of sympathy that vibrates throughout successive social networks. They remind us that the capacity to mend and the capacity to make whole both fall along points on a wide continuum, encompassing much more than just those self-consciously identified with the healing professions.

Of course, Swedenborg has something to say about healing and spiritual consciousness, as well. Swedenborg's conception of the spiritual personality embodies all that is human. Heaven, Swedenborg contends, is a person. In *Heaven and Hell*, he describes heaven as being made up of all the angelic societies—some constituting the arms and legs, others the head and heart, and so on. These, we have said, are made up of all the spirits in angelic form who have ever lived. At the same time, the living are to one degree or another angelic with regard to their interior being. All that is spiritual, in other words, is embodied in our humanity.

This Swedenborgian conception of the highest or most evolved personality has been called the Divine Natural Humanity. This is the manifestation of the holy not simply in the way we see ourselves, but in human relationships. The path to God is through our own interiors; yes, but this is not an isolated connection. The Divine is in the face of every human being. Our obligation, therefore, is not to turn from the world of others, but to become more fully engaged in human relationships, where consciousness, spirit, and humanity become one.

12

The Obligation
of the Healed

One of the basic postulates underlying a psychology of spiritual experience is that, when we are healed, there is a fundamental transformation that takes place in personality. Our symptoms have not been alleviated so that we can go back to the way we were thinking and behaving prior to our illness. Rather, we are no longer the person who we were before. In a sense, if we have been saved from physical death, we have died anyway because we die to our previous personality. Psychologically, our attitudes change: what we love is different; our entire outlook is transformed. We see with new eyes. We are born as another person in the sense that we have grown beyond who we once were and we have now moved into an entirely new sphere of psychic functioning. A physician who once heard a series of lectures on this subject said that he was sure everyone else could see the change in his attitude—scrawled across his forehead in large letters, he believed, was emblazoned the word "Appreciation."

It may be a sense that we have been granted a new life when before there was no hope. It could be that a dark time suddenly gave way to light. It may feel as if a great burden has been lifted from our shoulders. Now there is clarity when before there was uncertainty; now there is relief, when before there was suffering and anguish that seemed unending. In any event, we are not as we were before. The overarching emotion that we experience I would call gratitude. We are grateful for even the smallest things now: for the sound of another's voice, for the touch of another's hand, for the look from another face.

On recovery from one of those dark wanderings of the soul, a friend of mine once reported that he remembered one morning smelling a waft of spring air while sleeping near an open window, not yet awake, yet not asleep. There were many smells at once, yet all were alive, like grass, dirt, pollen, as if he were out on a farm near cows, even though this was in the city. He had smelled these scents before so many other times in his life. Yet now, he felt that the whole world was rolled up in that one waft of air, and he knew for certain at that minute that, when he died, he would never smell that smell of earth again. He was grateful to be able to smell it just then in more ways than he could ever communicate in words. At that moment, to him, his own mortality was most evident.

And with gratitude comes selflessness. When we look within, we no longer see just our physical life, or our sensual wants, or the material self. We see instead worlds within worlds, dimensions of consciousness yet to be explored, farther reaches into eternity in which our spirit is linked to all others. As we actualize our own humanity, humanity is transformed before us. To the extent that we lose our old self, to that extent we find ourselves in others. The more deeply we penetrate within, the more deeply we penetrate into the fabric of all who have ever lived. To have seen God, to have been in the presence of that great light, to have witnessed the Divine is to have seen the Divinely Human.

Indeed, when we have such experiences, they are often followed by a renewed commitment to our internal work. Previously, we may have dabbled in interior exploration, have accidentally stumbled through the inner door, have gotten just a glimpse of the beyond. Now, however, in the presence of absolute truth, we are confronted with the magnitude of the spiritual task that lies before us. We may have been caught totally unprepared to see what is divinely good, in the same way that we are never prepared to face absolute evil. We have been taught to beware always of the forces of evil, of course, but sometimes pure goodness can also have a devastating effect. The highest and most divine goodness can blind us if we have undergone limited development, or we are not yet ready to be in its presence. We must enter into the interior chamber nonetheless and emerge without having been completely destroyed by the experience.

There are also those moments in the midst of ecstasy when we are overcome by sheer terror. At such times, it is not uncommon to utter promises that become lifelong tasks to keep, if we can just survive that experience. Here we have the origin of ethical behavior, of duty to higher principles, of devotion to spiritual causes. In a spiritual sense, we experience a kind of creative fear, an awareness that the forces around us are much larger, more looming, and potentially greater than we can deal with; yet we may exist in some delicate balance with them, neither controlling that which is greater than ourselves nor being totally controlled by such forces. From such experiences, we learn a healthy skepticism about the spiritual life. For once having seen it, there are obligations that now descend upon us, obligations to ourselves and for the sake of all others.

In the aftermath of spiritual healing, we may also experience an overwhelming sense of loving presence. We may experience love for the world, for all that grows, for even the inanimate. This love, however—the consecration of the affections, the evolution of self-love and earthly love to new heights of spiritual feeling beyond any we had ever known—does tend toward a certain direction. It tends toward a life of the spirit, toward all sentient beings, living or dead. In the aftermath of spiritual awakening, Swedenborg suggests, evolves love for the neighbor, in whom we now see nothing less than the Divine Human.

In the wake of being healed, there is only one question: "What can I do now with my life, except live in service to others?" Henceforth, we now know, there is only one way to conduct ourselves, one course to set, one star to follow. This is the path of selflessness, of planetary service, of a life dedicated to higher spiritual causes. In such dedication is the power to effect healing in others through prayer from a distance, to alter the conditions of the moment so that the hidden spiritual meaning of things becomes evident, to assist others both materially and psychologically because we now know the higher spiritual purpose of even the lowest of material things.

Swedenborgians call this aftereffect of spiritual awakening the doctrine of uses.[1] Use is the herb-yielding seed, for all truths end in usefulness. Our first thoughts of how to be of use are the beginnings of regeneration, while, in the end, the internal spiritual personality is formed by God to perform his uses. Spirits and angels are known by the forms of their uses, just as the intentions of human beings are revealed in their actions. After all, what is the wisdom of higher spiritual teachings and the love of God and the neighbor if not to find some useful working out of these attributes in the world, some practical application in everyday life.

There are also, Swedenborg proposed, degrees of uses depending on spiritual purpose and ultimate effect in the world. The purpose of a broom is to sweep the room clean, but the occasion can also be an opportunity to sweep away unclean habits or to overcome sloth and torpor. To sweep our interior rooms clean could mean to empty out egotism in preparation for a filling up of spiritual knowledge. It could mean banishing from consciousness all thoughts that hinder us from spiritual liberation.

The question is, of course, how do we know when an object is nothing more than it seems. The answer lies in context. Swedenborg answered by saying that, in the spiritual world, communication is effected directly without the mediating use of words, and the level of spiritual intention—that is, the degree of use—is known and understood immediately. In the world of the merely human, we hear only to the depth and the height that we are able. As a young boy, when I heard my mother say, "Pass the salt" at the dinner table, I knew she meant to give her just the salt. However, when my father said, "Pass the salt," I understood that he meant to give him both the salt and the pepper. I had to know who was asking in order to know what to do. Sometimes the phrase "pass the salt," if uttered menacingly between two people who had been feuding, means "I am still angry." If it is the first communication after a week of not speaking to each other, it may be a gesture of reconciliation meaning, "I am now ready to begin talking with you again."

Similarly, when our intention has a high spiritual purpose, common phrases take on deeper and wider meanings. To have awakened is to be able to see into the spiritual reality of others and to speak to them at the level of their own awakening or to be spoken to in the same manner in return. This is a curious phenomenon, much like walking through a crowd looking into the faces of each person. In some, we see complete blankness, while, in other faces, we experience a shocking recognition because we see places we have been or may be on our way to, depending on how open we are to seeing and how open they are to letting us see in. It is easy for two strangers who meet briefly on a train or an airplane to reveal their inmost souls to each other in just a few short hours and then go their separate ways, never to meet again.

The doctrine of use, then, is the acting out of spiritual purpose in the material lives of others. It is the flow of divine energy into the world of the otherwise mundane. It is the revelation of spirit in nature, the actualization of spiritual wisdom using the conditions fashioned out of the immediate moment. It is the application of self-knowledge to the solution of practical problems in daily life. It is the test of our beliefs by observing their consequences.

This has profoundly important implications, if we would just think about it. The true end of all thought, all belief, all experience, is use. There may be a reality to the unseen, and the source of this unseen may be the spiritual dimension Swedenborg claimed; but its most direct manifestation is in the here-and-now, in the immediate moment, in concrete lives. The completion of the cycle is not a narcissistic turning inward so that our salvation is assured while that of others remains uncertain. Rather, it is the actualization of personal destiny through human relationships. The deepest and most holy embodiment of divinity is to be found in our connection to others.

We have already said that the core of all healing is belief, especially in terms of the compatibility between healer and patient. We must also consider the larger problem, however, of how people of mutually incompatible beliefs can interact to create a world that is more self-actualized, more realized, more fully conscious than the one we have known in the past. We are all painfully familiar with world wars, genocide, ethnic cleansing, famine, disease, and violent death in our world today. Where is the place we can create for our children that somehow does not repeat these recurring disasters? What is it that we need to do to bring about a world enlightenment? What kind of an environment would it be where suffering was lessened and healing nurtured?

One small step might be to consider that a world of preventative healing cannot come about as long as we think of sameness in terms of commonality of belief. All people might not have to believe the same thing in order to live together harmoniously. In fact, exactly the opposite might be the case. In order to appreciate diversity, in order to promote the uniqueness of the individual's quest for self-understanding, in order preserve the right of each person to find his or her own path, it may be that we must learn to acknowledge that spirituals truths can come from any source, any quarter, any root. As Jesus said in the Sermon on the Mount, "by their fruits you will know them."

In this maxim, we have the Swedenborgian doctrine of use, namely, beliefs that each person holds about the ultimate nature of reality should be judged not by their source but by their effect. To judge whether or not a belief is true or false for us, we must first test its validity by whether or not it works. On this basis, unless we are blind followers, we add and subtract from our belief system whatever knowledge we get from others or what we discover within ourselves.

What we do with the beliefs of others that do not work for us, however, is another matter. By rejecting those beliefs, we often reject the believer. No stronger message of hatred and ignorance is communicated to people than to suggest that their beliefs mean nothing and that their selfhood is meaningless. Meanwhile, no more important message is communicated to another when we acknowledge their reality and appeal to the highest and most inward dimension of their spiritual nature. Our penchant is to believe that everyone must subscribe to the same catechism, while the answer may be that radically different sources of spiritual knowledge may lead to the same consensually validated way of behaving.

In one sense, all relationships are spiritual relationships. If we relate to others through our interiors, we appeal constantly to the spiritual dimension of each person we encounter. The only way to have a personal relationship with the Divine is to have personal relationships with other human beings. But at any given minute, we plunge only to the depth that we are able. Purity of intention, the amount of egotistical involvement, our own blindness in believing that we know more than we do are but some of the factors constantly at work defining the kinds of relationships we will have with others.

In *Conjugial Love*, Swedenborg refers to these spiritual relationships as *conjugialis*, the marriage of souls.[2] He says that during earthly life we have many kinds of relationships. We marry the person whom we believe is our true mate, but this can only be validated in the spirit realm. For the discrepancy between the natural and the spiritual means that we may be connected to people in worldly ways, but there is no true bond in heaven. Spiritual relationships are based on the marriage of souls in heaven. Whoever has this connection gravitates together after death, so that each spirit is with the ones he or she loves the most. Such bonds form the basis of spiritual marriages in heaven after death, and also constitute the various societies of angels that make up the Divine Human.

Swedenborg also has much to say about the relation of the sexes to each other. While there are many points unique to his system, the issue is a universal one across religions and worldviews. Regardless of the differences, a common theme is that relationships are the basis for all healing. Think of the mother administering to the sick child, the nurse tending the wounded, the doctor and his ward of patients. And there are those that assist us on the path to self-realization—our teachers, gurus, mentors, and guides. Swedenborg himself was not alone in his quest, even though he apparently was a disciple of no one great spiritual teacher and he never married.

It is clear from Swedenborg's dream journal, however, that the process of internal spiritual transformation is grounded in an encounter between the gender opposites. Jungians speak of the male turning within and encountering the repressed feminine side of personality, while the female encounters the repressed and undeveloped masculine side that has been submerged.[3] Meeting this other represents a direct confrontation between consciousness and the unconscious.

The struggle that ensues begins by dislodging the dominant personality type from its fixed position. Maleness and femaleness then go into a state of flux, as the person begins to explore dimensions of consciousness beyond the waking state that also define personality. This, of course, goes quite beyond men's learning parenting skills and women's succeeding in the workforce. We are talking not about the social construction of gender identity, but the spiritual meaning of gender. An exploration of different states of consciousness means an encounter with the full spectrum of possible states. Fixation on any one of them produces only the fruits of that condition, and no more. Evolution through them, despite the dangers, constitutes the process of spiritual growth.

All the major esoteric traditions address in some way this transmutation of opposites. Deities are depicted in both their masculine and feminine form. Rama and Sita, Avalokateshvara and Kwan yin, even to a certain degree, Jesus and Mary are at different times venerated. In their respective traditions, the gendered opposites seem to take on the very qualities of a Brahma, Buddha, or Christ.

Self-knowledge must always be understood in the context of individuation, however. The goal in Tibetan Buddhism is expressed as *yuganadha*, the interaction and integration of the opposites as well as their transcendence. What the person becomes after liberation is then the question. One school of Zen contends that "before enlightenment—chopping wood, carrying water; after enlightenment—chopping wood, carrying water." In yoga, it is the *kaivalyin*, one who has mastered at will the ability to isolate consciousness from lifeless inert matter. In the Mahayana tradition of Buddhism, it is the *bodhisattva*, one who can become liberated at any time, but who vows instead to return to the world of suffering and help all sentient beings, down to the last blade of grass, pass over first. The liberated personality for the Sufis is far advanced from the normal personality, which is depicted as a wild horse or an untamed dog. Instead of destroying who we are in the natural world, however, they believe that the normal should be trained to a higher purpose.

What is the fundamental relationship of people to each other in this process of personal transformation? The least we can say is that no one is apart from this relationship, so that it is always within this context that healing takes place. In his work *Pragmatism*, William James took the position that we are not all connected to each other all of the time, but we are all interconnected.[4] By this he meant that any individual may have thirty-five or so relationships of one kind or another at any given moment, each one representing a different part of oneself; and, over time, these relationships keep changing. It is through the constantly changing patterns of relationships that people have an effect on each other, and there is a larger whole that is always affected by actions of the individual parts. James believed that each one of us has capacities to develop for good or ill. To the extent that we fail to actualize our potential, we hurt the progress of others. To the extent that we do actualize it, other lives are similarly enhanced.

We may likewise conclude that our obligation as the healed is to do our best to actualize our own capacities because this effort is the most important contribution we can make to the lives of others. At the same time, spiritual purpose is achieved when we can assist all other living beings toward spiritual self-realization.

13

Victory over Death

No more controversial question exists for us today than "What is death?" For the scientist, death means the cessation of all living processes, after which there is nothing. Religious traditions around the world have long held that death is an entry into new life and that the spirits of the dead live on in various forms. Swedenborg maintained that the effect of living in a body for a lifetime persists after death, so that on the after-death plane, we continue to see ourselves as embodied, except in a form more perfect than before. Christians hold that the souls of the dead shall rise again on Judgment Day, when each shall be judged according to its merit. Swedenborg took this prophecy to mean that we already lay sleeping in the physical body through our ignorance that spirit is the source of everything and that the term "Judgment Day" means spiritual awakening. When we finally see that matter is a manifestation of spirit, we are then able to enter into the spiritual world at will, converse with the angels, all while we are still in the physical body.

The significance of this view is that it equates the after-death plane with immediate exploration of internal states, as if an opening of the interior spiritual sense were preparation for what to expect beyond death's door. The interesting point is, however, that one's conception of death then also undergoes a change from the annihilation of life to something else, such as the transition from one state of consciousness to another. How much interior exploration while still in our body shows us the actual condition of the after-death plane is also uncertain.

While medical science is absolutely committed to preserving life, delaying death, slowing down the aging process, and otherwise seeking a form of living eternity, spiritualists of various kinds in many cultures have endeavored to return the dead to life, to awaken them back into the physical body, or at least to hear their voices again from beyond the grave.[1] Some social scientists, meanwhile, have concentrated on the near-death experience as a way to get as close as consciousness can to describing what is beyond that veil. The difficulty here, of course, in my opinion, is that no matter how long the person has been declared clinically dead and no matter what is communicated upon resuscitation, both researcher and subject still must operate on this side of the equation to conceptualize what has happened. All such reports presume that the after-death experience at the moment of transition can be rationally known; I, for one, am not sure that is the case. It may be that interior exploration while still in our physical body or that near-death experiences provide us with new forms of knowledge and dramatically change our views about physical life. But this still does not say that what is communicated there is the actual after-death experience. This is not to belittle such experiences, however, only to give greater emphasis to the process of spiritual self-realization in this life, which is what I believe these experiences are actually for.

With the exception of one major near-death experience of my own when I was a year-and-a-half, which I do not consciously remember, I led an otherwise extraordinarily sheltered childhood with regard to the death experience. I did not confront the issue until I was a graduating senior in high school, when my grandfather died at the age of 79.

My grandfather had been sequestered for two or three years in a rest home right across from the school, but I went to see him rarely. He had lived with me in my room at home the year before he entered the facility across the street from the school because there was no where else for him to go and my mother and father were determined to try to help him in his last days. It was an extraordinarily difficult year that we lived together, since his mental faculties were slipping even faster than his physical ones. It was getting difficult for him to remember even his immediate family; and when he lost the ability to control his bodily functions, it was obvious that he needed twenty-four-hour-a-day care that we could not give as a family. His situation stabilized once he was moved to the rest home, but I had to invent any number of reasons for visiting him, since he did not always know who I was. I had never known him very well when I was growing up, and these were difficult conditions at best in which to start up a relationship.

I remember that I was in my last-period class, American History, when the phone call came. The message the teacher communicated to me was "go over right away after school." Unfortunately, the real message was "come over right away, right now." As a result, my grandfather died just a few minutes before I arrived. Things moved very quickly as soon as I walked in the door, however. My mother asked me if I wanted to go in to see him. I had not particularly thought about it, but, under the circumstances, conjectured that perhaps this was some kind of custom I had not been told about, so reflexively I said, "Yes."

The nurse led me into the room where my grandfather had stayed with eight other patients. They were all still there, in various states of mental and physical de composition, and so was he. His bed was there like all the others, except now surrounded by a screen. The nurse stood by the entrance to the screen and motioned me in. In an instant, she was gone, and I was standing there by his bedside. He was definitely dead. I felt his hand and got hard bone and cold flesh. His eyes were closed, but his mouth was slightly open, since the nurses had taken out his false teeth long ago. I think they were in a glass of water by the bed.

As I stood there, I searched for the man I knew but could not find him localized any longer in that physical body. I felt his presence, yet it was nowhere immediately to be found. Under the circumstances, I decided to surrender myself to the moment; and as I did, I felt my consciousness expanding to the farther reaches of everything I had known and just kept going. I had an experience that was wider and deeper and farther out than any I had experienced up to that moment. It was like a peak experience in which I felt that the moment was more real than most other moments I had ever lived through. I felt that, in my search, my grandfather was in all those places. He was at once everywhere and nowhere. I had found him, yet he was nowhere to be physically discovered. I felt as if a veil had been lifted, and I was permitted to see a larger view of reality, which to this day remains with me.

This experience helped me tremendously in the days that followed. The wake, the funeral, and the burial were all important, but much smaller in significance than what I had experienced at the bedside. There were tears, of course, but much unexpected humor, and also the realization of a small dose of wisdom.

Building on that experience, over the years I have come to reflect on the importance of seeing beyond the bounds of waking consciousness. An expansion of consciousness, a deepening of perception, a more subtle kind of clarity now seemed possible. Consciousness was malleable; it did not always just stay the same from birth to death. It had a multitude of varieties across the life span. It expanded and contracted. It came in waves. I was much more cavalier about it when I was younger, in the days when I was teenager and thought, like many young people, that I was immortal. I went through many phases, believing that I knew about the nature of reality, that I was practicing disciplines that would help me overcome the fear of death, that I was somehow privileged to see what I had seen. Now, however, that I am older and have visited death's door so many more times through friends, relatives, and acquaintances, I am much less certain about some things and yet absolutely certain about others. Perhaps the one most common theme to emerge, however, is the idea that victory over death is not necessarily always a question of physical survival.

To contact departed loved ones, for instance, seems absolutely impossible in today's scientific world—a fantasy, a superstition debunked long ago by scientists, physicians, psychologists and even many of the clergy. Yet every culture in the world except our modern one maintains that departed spirits on the after-death plane do, in fact, communicate everyday with the living. Nowhere is this more pronounced than in popular Taoism, one of the great religious traditions of China.

Recently, for instance, I attended the sixteenth international Yan Zin Chi Kung conference, held in Boston for the benefit of the one thousand ethnic Chinese who attended. I had been invited as a guest to come to the opening lecture, held in a large hall, and to attend three days of workshops put on in a nearby hotel, workshops that lasted 18-1/2 hours each day. Aside from my own general interest in Chinese culture, at one point in my earlier career, I had surveyed the major texts of Confucianism and Taoism and read several summaries of the history of Chinese philosophy. I had also been practicing the Japanese martial art of aikido for some twenty-five years, and I knew that aikido, the Japanese art of blending with energy, and *tai chi*, the traditional Chinese Taoist movement exercises for health and longevity, were related through the development of *chi*, meaning energy or spirit. So, I was not totally unprepared for what I was about to experience.

Essentially, we were taught trance fasting and visualization to communicate with the ancestors. As I have said, Chinese culture accepts the reality of life after death, and the cult of ancestor worship is still very strong in China. Ancestor worship means constant and daily veneration of the elders, so that the affairs of the family are always in proper order. It also means devotion to the dead, especially in the form of the family shrine in the home. In the Chinese Taoist pantheon no individual ever acts alone, for every act performed in secret is witnessed by the successive generations of one's family who are always there in the spirit world, continually looking on. At the same time, no decision is ever made by the individual in isolation, as the ancestors are perpetually there for moral guidance as well as spiritual inspiration.

The workshop proceeded through a long train of introductions. Two microphones were going at once throughout, one in Chinese and one in English. Occasionally, another Chinese dialect would join in an asynchronized chorus, creating the conditions for dissociated consciousness. Instructions were then begun, including those in meditation. In particular, trance visualizations, where the individual sees him- or herself within the enfolding arms of the family, were practiced. Other instructions were to meditate on the faces of the mother and the father, especially in their best and most healthy aspect. Such exercises were also accompanied by spontaneous bodily movements of an automatic nature, and the utterance of any kind of sounds that might make audible the unique state of consciousness the person was experiencing. There were also periodic group exercises of specific physical postures in Chinese yoga and also training in breathing techniques. Questions were posed, and answers were given, as were testimonials. Cathartic public confessions, such as one would hear in an AA group, also continued periodically throughout the weekend.

During one of these question periods, an American man asked the teacher about what happens to one's experience if one has recently lost one's parents. His had both died recently within a few months of each other. I, too, was interested in this question, since I was still going through the grief of the then-recent death of my own father from cancer. The teacher answered that such persons are actually closer to the core of the visualization experience than others who had not experienced a recent death.

During one of the few breaks that were permitted, I went home. During one of these times I had occasion to call my mother, and I received a message from the dead. Without any knowledge that I had been going to the Chi Kung conference, she announced that she had been going through the family strong box just that morning and had come across something my father had written on a pad, apparently just moments before he died. It was a brief message, with the time on it, just describing the intensity of the pain he was experiencing at that moment—a synchronous event, to be sure.

On another of these breaks, I called my eleven-year-old son, who was separated from me at that time by some two thousand miles. I knew we were lonely for each other, and he was having a hard time adjusting to the circumstance he was in, so I called to tell him about the workshop. He was interested, so we tried an experiment. He took the portable phone to his room and lay down on the bed. I told him to try to sense my presence right next to him so that he could call it forth whenever he needed me. I took him through some of the steps we had been practicing for breathing, meditation, and relaxation, then took him into the visualization state.

After some minutes, suddenly he said he felt me right there next to him. Simultaneously, however, his best friend Nick, from whom he was also separated by two thousand miles, appeared. While all this was going on, he was lying on his bed with the portable phone in his ear, and I was standing in my kitchen leaning against the counter. Then, just as he was reporting that his friend had appeared right there beside him, along with me, I turned to my left in my own kitchen and saw my father standing there next to me. All of these visualizations, both planned and unplanned, appeared at the same instant, two on his end of the phone and one on mine.

I distinctly remember the look on my father's face as being youthful and healthy. He was dressed in a fashionable suit and tie, with new shoes and a fresh haircut. There was some communication, some exchange between the two of us, but I was not aware of any words actually being spoken. Meanwhile, as I stood there, I was having a running commentary with my son on the phone about what was happening to him two thousand miles away. After a short time, I hung up and went back to continue the seminar.

A week later I had the same experience. I was driving by myself over a considerable distance. At a certain point, I looked over, and there I saw my father sitting in the passenger seat. He looked over at me, and we again had an exchange. I do not remember the content, only that it pertained to something I was thinking about at the moment.

The lesson in this for me is that the spiritual connection between the generations in my family could be strengthened through adversity, separation, and loss. It also seems to me that this link is eternal, transcending even death.

But did he really come back? Was it really him? Wasn't I just hallucinating? This is like asking, "Did Don Juan really exist as a man in the flesh?" Or, "What did Joseph Campbell really mean when he said 'Follow your bliss?'" Such questions do not really have any meaning for someone who has experienced the relativity of one state of consciousness in relation to another. They are only asked by pundits of high culture who have never seen the other side. That passage from the physical body to the spiritual is a momentous event. My predilection is to see that there is some inherent relation between transcendence and the experience of death, and that self-realization, an awakening to a higher spiritual consciousness, constitutes the great victory over a return to physical survival on the earthly plane.

I am reminded of an instance of this that puzzled me because it showed how difficult it is, especially in circumstances where illness draws the process out interminably, to adjust to the inevitability of death, both for the dying and those who remain behind. A 41-year-old woman who, with her husband, had been trying to conceive a child under the care of a physician, received a tragic diagnosis of breast cancer. After surgery, chemotherapy, and radiation, the woman was on the mend, with family, friends, and coworkers all supporting a succession of big lifestyle changes. One of these was that the couple took up a strict macrobiotic diet, which everyone willingly accommodated.

Within a year, however, the cancerous growth returned and began to metastasize. The couple's situation appeared to be taking a grim turn; but, at the same time, their circle of friends noticed a tremendous deepening of the relationship between the two of them. Both seemed to grow as people and to find in each other a loving sense of presence. In the woman's final weeks, the two came to a profound agreement. It was more of an unspoken pact than a verbal exchange; the actual words were less important than the inner spiritual meaning of what they were trying to say to each other. She promised not to push him away if he promised not to be angry with her for leaving. He promised to be there for her until the very end, if she promised to let him. He promised to see that she was comfortable and free from pain; she promised to bear whatever happened so they could remain together. Simply, love would take them.

The difficulty was that as their bond grew stronger and more exclusive, other relatives were pushed away, particularly the woman's mother. This was a most difficult phase of the woman's passage, because every time the mother came to see her in the hospital, all the unresolved issues between them came up. Foremost was that the woman had reconciled herself with her own death, but the mother still clung to life. It was an existential situation that could not be resolved. The mother's visits became more upsetting, until the daughter finally asked to say good-bye, which the mother just could not fathom. Their differences were too far apart; they could not find a place to meet, and the mother did not come again. When the woman finally died a few weeks later, her husband was there by her bedside.

This episode helps us to understand that not death itself but being able to make the transition may be the more difficult task. For those we leave behind, our death could be the final straw that breaks them and causes them to give up all hope in this world. Many cases exist where longtime partners are reunited in death within just a few months, or parents lose a child and never fully recover.

On the other hand, such a personal loss can be the springboard for transcendence and renewal. Here is the case of a forty-two-year-old woman who had just lost her father and, overwhelmed in a sea of emotion, had been struggling with grief. After several months had passed, the woman received a sign through her dreams, which she took to be both a mythic description of and a healing reconciliation with what had happened. In her description, she aptly describes in visionary terms what phenomenologically she conceives as the domain of the spirit:

> I grew unbearably exhausted this afternoon so
> I just gave it up and got into bed for a nap. I
> proceeded to have a dream which is right up

there among the most stunning I've ever had. I was with Dad, and we were clearly "in his current reality." The setting was a beautiful golf course with greens so intense words can't describe the colors. It was like a regular golf course in every other sense, except that instead of atmosphere, there was golden light infusing everything. It was as if the place had a halo because light was everywhere the golf course wasn't. We were just walking and talking . . . enjoying being together. It wasn't a dream with conversation, per se, just "beingness." At some point the purpose of our visit became clear—he was showing me where he is, and what he now knows. To demonstrate it, suddenly we were scanning humans—none whose faces were significant, but it was implied that they were people like those I share my life with. Just people. But instead of their personalities being dominant, their spirits were what could be discerned . . . or rather, the essential nature of humans, which was totally pure, unconditional, intense love that was pure intention and filled with longing, caring, and connectedness. The love was so big, so deep, so intense that it was painful to observe, and I seem to recall groaning, or heaving, and I may have even had to turn my head away. . . . The implication was, "Here I am, this is who I know all of us [humans] to be. This is who we are as the personality and ego fall away. This is the reality I want you to have a look at, to be peaceful about, and try to attain if you wish, . . . but that isn't the point, really. This is merely who we really are. Without human form, no effort is required." It was like, "don't worry—this is who you are whether you know it or not. Not knowing it won't change a thing, but knowing it might get you consciously connected with it a little faster." It was like peeking behind the curtain, or the mask, and discovering the magnificent creation of which we are a part.[2]

Shortly after her father died, one of her best friends died also. In losing these dearest people, she says, and so closely together, she has learned "that the fragrance of death is love, and that by confounding the mind, death takes consciousness to spiritual levels of experience that otherwise would not be discovered."

This brings me to the final question: is there such a thing as good death? One at first might not be able to imagine it possible; but I think that physicians, nurses, healers, hospice workers, the clergy, and others who minister to the dying would have some extraordinary things to tell us if asked to address this question.

One account came from the family of a 76-year-old man, a devout Catholic but definitely an independent thinker, father of four children, with a loving wife and a large circle of devoted relatives, friends, and acquaintances. He had worked outside as a lineman all his life, as an employee of the state electric company. He had not seen a doctor in fifty years, since his discharge from the navy as a young man, had never been sick, and had never taken so much as even an aspirin during that time.

Then one day, while on a vacation with his family in New Hampshire, he lost his speech and his ability to walk. A stroke was at first suspected; but, subsequently, x-rays and a CAT scan at a local hospital revealed a brain tumor. Deferring to the concern of his family, he agreed to enter a major university teaching hospital where specialists could make a more precise diagnosis. At that point, he was put on five different types of medication, including anticonvulsants, a drug for a condition unrelated to the brain tumor, and drugs to counter the effect of other drugs—a nurse had to begin daily administration of insulin, because some of his medication created a diabetic condition, a byproduct of treatment.

The effect of the situation was to throw the immediate family into a panic, as they moved their lives into a crisis mode. Within the first ten days, the family's most immediate problem was that both the man and his wife could not sleep. However, the physicians were not able to give sleep medication because this would interfere with the anticonvulsants. The specialists looked at the x-rays and the CAT scans and diagnosed the tumor as a rare glioma, with diffuse degeneration of the brain tissues also occurring.

A biopsy was planned that would require an overnight stay in the hospital. If the tumor were slow growing, radiation therapy might stop it completely; if fast growing, then no intervention would be of help. Meanwhile, the man's demeanor had improved; he had regained his speech, although slowed, and he could walk, but haltingly. He walked into the hospital under his own steam, but was quickly shunted into the passive patient mode, asked to don the johnny-open-in-the-back, and confined to bed awaiting the procedure, all of which, to the nurses' delight, he good-humoredly resisted. The procedure involved drilling a dime-shaped hole in his head, after which the physicians went into the deep part of the brain and took a sample of the tumor that could be tested in the laboratory. The anesthetic was local, so he remained conscious, chatting with the doctors throughout. When the procedure was over, the doctors declared "Okay, all through." Not being acquainted with proper hospital procedure, the man thought that meant he could go. He started to get up off the surgical table and walk away by himself, again to the amusement of the nurses, until he was gently restrained. The next day, the family came and the doctor discharged him from the hospital. A head nurse came in just as they were leaving, however, and tried to have him readmitted for an extra day of rehabilitation. The family thanked her but said they had no intention of staying in the hospital, and they went home. The results of the pathological report a few days later were grim, however. The tumor was fast growing, and the prognosis was that the father had only months, perhaps just weeks left. The physician said the man's mental capacities would remain clear, but he would stop walking and speaking soon. He was encouraged to re-enter the hospital, but declined. Instead, he wanted to be home, to be with his family, where he could be in his own bed, in his own room, with his favorite pictures of children and grandchildren and paintings of Jesus, and with those whom he loved around him.

The man died just twelve weeks later. In the interim, one of the most extraordinary of human events took place. First, a steady stream of people began to come by to pay homage to a very simple but very great man. It was as if the doors to the collective unconscious were opened and the family got to see people whom they had not seen for a long time, in some cases, decades. There was reunion, renewal, and reverence by day, and the ever-constant family vigil by night. Certainly, there were phases to his decline. There was much expression of sorrow, but very little evidence of organic pain. He declined gracefully and with all the dignity such a person deserved. He did not want to be a prolonged burden on his family, who struggled to understand how best to help transition him out. There were also numerous chances for young and old alike who were very close to him to say good-bye.

During those weeks, serendipitous events took place one after another for the family, time was suspended, visionary images of deep personal meaning to different individuals would recur—in all there was a vast collective recounting of the saga of this man's life. He apparently had left no unfinished business; he was sure each one of his family was safe, and each family member was absolutely certain where he would be going. There were no doctors present at the end, just the family and the hospice workers, who said that it was the most peaceful and uncomplicated death they had ever seen.

Afterwards, there was no autopsy. No study was undertaken of his rare tumor, no journal article was written. The significance of this event was that this man and his family in their own way had solved one of the great questions of modern medicine. When is a patient really dead? How important is the transition, really? He had chosen to walk away from the healthcare system at the end and die in the arms of his loving family. The victory they achieved was that man-made circumstances came back into their control so that the larger cosmic ones could play themselves out according to their own natural consequence.

In all these examples, the idea of healing takes on a completely new meaning. Healing is associated with consciousness. Healing can mean wound healing, yes; but it also means the resolution of personal problems, even the actualization of personal destiny. When experience takes on these dimensions, the traditional ways in which we have framed illness, disease, infirmity, and death become transformed. Personality becomes something else—higher, deeper, wider, and more encompassing than mere science can articulate. Science, after all, is our tool, but not the reason for life itself. We need constant reminding that, despite all plausible explanations from the rational intellect, the larger mystery of who we are and why we are here remains before us, unanswered. Perhaps blessedly so.

Notes

ℰ Introduction ℐ

1. Eugene Taylor, "Psychological Suspended Animation: Heart Rate, Blood Pressure, Time Estimation, and Introspective Reports from an Anechoic Environment" (Master's thesis, Department of Psychology, Southern Methodist University, Dallas, Texas, 1973).

2. E. Taylor, "Contemporary Interest in Classical Eastern Psychology," in *Asian Contributions to Psychology*, ed. A. Paranjpe, D. Ho, and R. Rieber (New York: Praeger, 1988), 79–122.

3. For instance, see E. Taylor, "Transpersonal Psychology: Its Several Virtues," *The Humanistic Psychologist*, 20, nos. 2 and 3 (1992): 285–300.

4. E. Taylor, Ching-tse Lee, and J. Ding-E Young, "Bringing Mind-Body Medicine into the Mainstream," *Hospital Practice* 32, no. 5 (May 1997): 183–196.

5. See my article "Swedenborgianism," in *America's Alternative Religions*, ed. T. Miller (Albany, New York: SUNY Press, 1995).

6. See my chapter, "Ralph Waldo Emerson: The Swedenborgian and Transcendentalist Connection," in *Emanuel Swedenborg: A Continuing Vision*, ed. R. Larsen (New York: Swedenborg Foundation, 1988), 127–136; rpt. in *Testimony to the Invisible: Essays on Swedenborg*, ed. J. F. Lawrence (West Chester, Pennsylvania: Swedenborg Foundation, 1995), 140–171.

7. Wilson Van Dusen, *The Natural Depth in Man* (New York: Harper & Row, 1972; rpt. Swedenborg Foundation, 1981) and *The Presence of Other Worlds: The Psychological/Spiritual Findings of Emanuel Swedenborg* (New York: Harper & Row, 1974; rpt. Swedenborg Foundation, 1991).

8. E. Taylor, "Our Roots: The American Visionary Tradition," *Noetic Sciences Review* (Fall 1993): 1–12; and "Desperately Seeking Spirituality," *Psychology Today*, Nov. Dec. 1994, 56–91.

9. Keller's "spiritual autobiography" *My Religion*, first published in 1927, is no longer in print. However, recently it has been edited and enlarged by Ray Silverman and reissued under the title *Light in My Darkness* (West Chester: Swedenborg Foundation, 1994).

ℰ Chapter One ℐ

1. William James, *Principles of Psychology*, 2 vols. (New York: Henry Holt, 1890). See especially James's chapter on "The Stream of Thought,"

2. Larry Dossey, *Healing Words: The Power of Prayer and the Practice of Medicine* (San Francisco: Harper, 1973).

3. See Office of Alternative Medicine, *Alternative Medicine: Expanding Medical Horizons* (Washington, D.C.: GPO, 1993).

4. Mircea Eliade, *Shamanism: Archaic Techniques of Ecstasy*, trans. W. R. Trask (New York: Bollingen Foundation, 1964); Joseph Campbell, *Hero with a Thousand Faces* (New York: Pantheon Books, 1949); Henri Ellenberger, *Discovery of the Unconscious* (New York: Basic Books, 1970).

5. For background on this, see Basdeo Bissoondoyal, *The Essence of the Vedas and Allied Scriptures* (Bombay: Jaico Publishing House, 1966); and Shree Prohit Swami and W. B. Yeats, *The Ten Principal Upanishads* (London: Faber and Faber Ltd., 1937).

6. Thomas G. Dummer, *Tibetan Medicine and Other Holistic Health-Care Systems* (London: Routledge, 1988).

7. Richard Katz, *Boiling Energy* (Cambridge, Massachusetts: Harvard University Press, 1982).

8. Robert F. Heizer and M. A. Hipple, ed. *The California Indians: A Source Book* (Berkeley: University of California Press, 1971).

❧ Chapter Two ❧

1. Lama Anagarika Govinda, *The Psychological Attitude of Early Buddhist Philosophy and Its Systematic Representation according to Abhidhamma Tradition* (London: Rider, 1961).

2. Walter Houston Clark, *The Oxford Group: Its History and Significance* (New York: Bookman Associates, 1951).

3. C. G. Jung, *Psychology and Religion* (New Haven, Connecticut: Yale University Press, 1938).

4. Stanislav Grof, *Realms of the Human Unconscious* (New York: Viking, 1975).

5. Victor Frankl, *Man's Search for Meaning: An Introduction to Logotherapy*, trans. Ilse Lasch (Boston: Beacon Press, 1963).

6. Emanuel Swedenborg, *Divine Love and Wisdom*, trans. J. C. Ager (West Chester, Pennsylvania: 1885; rpt. Swedenborg Foundation, 1995).

7. Marguerite Block, *New Church in the New World* (New York: Swedenborg Publishing Association, 1984). Also, Samuel Hahnemann, *The Organon of Medicine*, 6th edition, trans. W. Boericke (New Delhi: B. Jain, 1997).

❦ Chapter Three ❧

1. Emanuel Swedenborg, *Arcana Coelestia*, 12 vols., trans. John Clowes, ed. and rvd. J. F. Potts, 2nd ed. (West Chester, Pennsylvania: Swedenborg Foundation, 1995 1998). The first volume has also been published as *Heavenly Secrets* (New York: Swedenborg Foundation, 1905).

❦ Chapter Four ❧

1. Elmer and Alyce Green, *Beyond Biofeedback* (New York: Delacorte Press/S. Lawrence, 1977).

2. John C. Lilly, *The Center of the Cyclone: An Autobiography of Inner Space* (New York: Julian Press, 1972).

3. Herbert Benson, *The Relaxation Response* (New York: Morrow, 1975); *Your Maximum Mind* (New York: Times Books, 1987); *Timeless Healing* (New York: Scribner's, 1996).

❦ Chapter Five ❧

1. Christopher Chapple, *The Yoga Sutras of Patanjali: An Analysis of the Sanskrit with Accompanying English Translation* (Delhi, India: Sri Satguru Publications, 1990).

2. Wilson Van Dusen, ed., *Emanuel Swedenborg's Journal of Dreams, 1743–1744* (New York: Swedenborg Foundation, 1986).

3. Eugene Taylor, *William James on Exceptional Mental States* (New York: Scribner's, 1982).

4. Patricia Garfield, *Creative Dreaming* (New York: Simon and Schuster, 1975).

5. Herbert Silberer, "Report on a Method of Eliciting and Observing Certain Symbolic Hallucination-Phenomena," in *Organization and Pathology of Thought*, ed. D. Rapaport (New York: Columbia University Press, 1965), 156–172.

6. Jeanne Achterberg, *Imagery in Healing: Shamanism and Modern Medicine* (Boston: New Science Library, Shambhala, 1985).

❦ Chapter Six ❧

1. F. W. H. Myers, *The Subliminal Consciousness, with an introduction by James Webb* (New York: Arno Press, 1976).

2. C. G. Jung, *Analytical Psychology: Its Theory and Practice* (London: Routledge & Kegan Paul, 1968).

3. For instance, see William Willoya and Vincent Brown, *Warriors of the Rainbow* (Healdsburg, California: Naturegraph Publishers, 1968).

4. Emanuel Swedenborg, *Divine Providence*, trans. William F. Wunsch, 2nd ed. (West Chester, Pennsylvania: Swedenborg Foundation, 1996); C. G. Jung, "Synchronicity: The Acausal Connecting Principal," in *The Interpretation of Nature and the Psyche*, trans. R. F. C. Hull and P. Silz (London: Routledge & Kegan Paul, 1955).

5. Printed with permission of the author.

❦ Chapter Seven ❧

1. Louis Renou, *Vedic India* (Calcutta: Susil Gupta, 1957).

2. See, for example, Huston Smith, *The Religions of Man* (New York: Harper, 1958).

3. Emanuel Swedenborg, *Heaven and Hell*, trans. John C. Ager, 2nd ed. (West Chester, Pennsylvania: The Swedenborg Foundation, 1995), paragraph 429.

4. *The Diagnostic and Statistical Manual of Mental Disorders*, 4th ed. (Washington, D.C.: American Psychiatric Association, 1994).

5. Freely adapted from Carl W. Ernst, "The Stages of Love in Early Persian Sufism, from Rab'a to Ruzbihan," in *Classical Persian Sufism from Its Origins to Rumi*, ed. L. Lewisohn (London: Khaniqahi Nimatullahi Publications, 1996), 435–455.

❧ Chapter Eight ❧

1. Swedenborg, *Arcana Coelestia*, paragraph 4627.

2. Shree Prohit Swami and W. B. Yeats, *The Ten Principal Upanishads* (London: Faber and Faber Ltd., 1937).

3. William James, "On Fechner," in *A Pluralistic Universe* (Cambridge, Massachusetts: Harvard University Press, 1977).

4. Jorge Luis Borges, "Testimony to the Invisible," in *Emanuel Swedenborg: A Continuing Vision*, ed. R. Larsen (New York: Swedenborg Foundation, 1988), 353.

❧ Chapter Nine ❧

1. William James, *The Varieties of Religious Experience* (New York: Longmans, 1902).

2. This and all further excerpts are printed with the author's permission.

3. Printed with permission of the author.

4. Swedenborg's Journal of Dreams, 46–48.

5. Gia Fu Feng and Jane English, *The Tao-Te-Ching* (New York: Vintage/Random House, 1997).

6. D. T. Suzuki, *Studies in Zen* (London: Unwin Paperbacks, 1986).

7. Emanuel Swedenborg, *The Last Judgment and Babylon Destroyed*, in *Miscellaneous Theological Works*, trans. John Whitehead, 2nd ed. (West Chester, Pennsylvania: Swedenborg Foundation, 1996).

❦ Chapter Ten ❧

1. Swedenborg, *Divine Love and Wisdom*, paragraph 1.

2. Josiah Royce, *The Philosophy of Loyalty* (New York: The MacMillan Company, 1908).

3. F. W. H. Myers, *Human Personality and Its Survival of Bodily Death*, 2 vols. (London: Longmans, Green, 1903).

4. Milton H. Erickson, *The Collected Papers of Milton H. Erickson on Hypnosis*, ed. E. L. Rossi (New York: Irvington Publishers, 1980); Jeffrey Zeig, *Experiencing Erickson: An Introduction to the Man and His Work* (New York: Brunner/Mazel, 1985).

❦ Chapter Eleven ❧

1. Swedenborg, *Heaven and Hell*, paragraph 528.

2. Those interested in reading more about the individuals I have chosen should see the following: Tenzing Norgay, with J. R. Ullman, *Tiger of the Snows: The Autobiography of Tenzing of Everest* (New York: Putnam [1955]); Elie Wiesel, *Against Silence: The Voice and the Vision of Elie Wiesel*, selected and edited by Irving Abrahamson, 3 vols. (New York: Holocaust Library, 1985); Harry J. Cargas, *Conversations with Elie Wiesel* (South Bend, Indiana: Justice Books, 1992); and Tenzin Gyatso, *Freedom in Exile: The Autobiography of the Dalai Lama* (New York: HarperCollins, 1990).

3. The historic event for the Swedenborgians, however, was an exchange of books. The officers of the Boston Tibetan Association had explained to the Dalai Lama how the Cambridge Society at the Swedenborg

Chapel had taken the Tibetans under its wing. The Church Council was then introduced to the Dalai Lama, who gave the Swedenborgians a signed copy of his autobiography, while the Swedenborgians offered in exchange copies of Swedenborg's *Divine Love and Divine Wisdom* and some other volumes. From this meeting, it was hoped that a dialogue could begin within the Swedenborgian community on world religions and between the Swedenborgians and the Tibetans on matters of most interest to the Dalai Lama, including the Tibetan experience in America and nonviolent means to free Tibet.

ℭ Chapter Twelve ℈

1. See *Divine Love and Wisdom.*

2. See Emanuel Swedenborg, *Conjugial Love*, trans. S. Warren, rvd. by L. Tafel (New York: Swedenborg Foundation, 1915). This work is also known as *Marital Love.* A recent translation is *Love in Marriage*, trans. David F. Gladish (New York: Swedenborg Foundation, 1992).

3. C. G. Jung, *Archetypes and the Collective Unconscious*, trans. R. F. C. Hull (New York: Pantheon Books, 1959).

4. William James, *Pragmatism* (New York: Longmans, 1907).

ℭ Chapter Thirteen ℈

1. Eugene Taylor, "Mortality and Self-Realization," in *Psychic Phenomena and Near-Death Experiences*, ed. J.

MacMahon (New York: Parapsychology Foundation, 1995).

2. Printed with permission of author.

Index

Borges, Jorge Luis, 113
Borysenko, Joan, xviii
Boston
  Cambodian refugees, 34
    Tibetan immigrants,
    161–163
brain waves, 67–68, 70
breath, control of, 72–73, 130
Buchman, Frank, 24
Buddha, 19, 135
Buddhism, 18, 33, 35, 129, 138,
  145
    Eightfold Path, 135
    First Turning of the Wheel,
    135
    Hinayana
      nibanna, 123, 127
      nirvana, 127
    Mahayana, 128
      bodhisattva, 158, 174
      sunyata, 126, 128
    Three Refuges, 135
    Tibetan, 14
      yuganadha, 174
    Zen
      kensho, 126
      koan, 144
      tongu zen shu, 129
      satori, 126
Bunyan, John, *Pilgrim's Progress*,
  90

C
Cabot, Richard C., xvi
Campbell, Joseph, 12, 86, 89,
  184
catabolism, 133
Catholicism, Roman, 21, 24
chaos theory, 139
chi, 91, 181
Christianity, 19, 24, 36, 126, 138,
  145
    Orisen, 126

Church of the New Jerusalem,
  xvii, 31, 104
citta, 106
Cobb, Stanley, xvi
concentration camps, 26, 160
confession, 25
Confucius, *Analects*, 135
consciousness, state(s) of, 2–16,
  19, 24, 25, 29, 35, 36, 37,
  42–43, 53, 55, 56, 62, 64, 65,
  68, 71, 72, 74, 75, 76, 79, 81,
  82, 83, 86, 89, 90, 92, 93, 95,
  101, 102, 103, 106, 113,
  115–118, 126–131, 132, 136,
  141, 145, 153, 160, 166, 174,
  177, 180, 184, 185, 188, 191
creativity, 141

D
Dalai Lama, 161–163
darshan, 19
Davis, Andrew Jackson, xix
death, 145–146, 176–178, 184,
  186, 188
Demeter, 89–90
depression, psychological,
  94–98, 137
dharma, 135–136
*Diagnostic and Statistical Manual,
  The*, (DSM), 93–94
Divine Providence, 139
Dossey, Larry, xviii, 11
dreams, interpretation of, 62, 72

E
Earth-Soul, doctrine of, 112, 114
egolessness, 152–154
Eliade, Mircea, 12, 90
Ellenberger, Henri, 12
Emerson, Ralph Waldo, xv, xvi,
  xix, 102, 110
Erickson, Milton, 141
Evans, Warren Felt, xix, 35

S

T

U

V

W